A Life God
REWARDS

DEVOTIONAL

A *Life God*
REWARDS
DEVOTIONAL

Bruce Wilkinson

with DAVID KOPP

Multnomah® Publishers *Sisters, Oregon*

A LIFE GOD REWARDS DEVOTIONAL
published by Multnomah Publishers, Inc.

© 2002 by Exponential, Inc.
International Standard Book Number: 1-59052-009-2
Cover image by Koechel Peterson & Associates

Italics in Scripture quotations are the author's emphasis.

Scripture quotations are from *The Holy Bible,* New King James Version.
© 1982 by Thomas Nelson, Inc. Used by permission.

Other Scripture quotations:

The Holy Bible, New International Version (NIV)
© 1973, 1984 by International Bible Society,
used by permission of Zondervan Publishing House

Multnomah is a trademark of Multnomah Publishers, Inc.,
and is registered in the U.S. Patent and Trademark Office.
The colophon is a trademark of Multnomah Publishers, Inc.
Printed in the United States of America

For information:
MULTNOMAH PUBLISHERS, INC.
POST OFFICE BOX 1720
SISTERS, OREGON 97759

02 03 04 05 06 07 08—10 9 8 7 6 5 4 3 2 1 0

CONTENTS

LIVING *for* GOD'S "WELL DONE!"

You could think of eternal reward as both the first and last thing on Jesus' mind. Consider…

When Jesus began His teaching ministry, His *first* major pronouncement was connected to a startling truth—that God will reward you in heaven for what you do for Him on earth. "Blessed are you…" He said in the Sermon on the Mount. "Rejoice and be exceedingly glad, for great is your reward in heaven" (Matthew 5:11–12). And the *last* major pronouncement of Jesus, recorded on the last page of the Bible, was on the same subject: "Behold, I am coming quickly, and My reward is with Me, to give to every one according to his work" (Revelation 22:12).

Why, then, has what Jesus revealed about the importance of our work for God been so overlooked in our generation? And at what cost to our present purpose and our future joy?

I wrote *A Life God Rewards* to help people recapture the truth about the connection between what we do today and what God will do for us in eternity, and, by His grace, to reignite a passion for serving Him in this life. If you haven't read the book yet, I urge you to do so.

The thirty-one-day devotional you're holding is designed to take you further in your understanding of what Jesus taught about rewards. The first three days review the central message of *A Life God Rewards,* then over the span of four weeks of readings, you'll gain fresh insight and motivation to make living for God's "Well done!" the most important measure of your life.

By all means pick up the companion tool, *A Life God Rewards Journal.* You'll find a helpful journal prompter incorporated with each day's entry. As so many spiritual pilgrims have discovered, the practice of writing down what you are learning and how you are changing can add tremendous impact to God's work in your life. Also, be sure to take advantage of the *A Life God Rewards Bible Study* and video seminar for further personal or group learning.

By the time you've finished this devotional, I'm confident you'll look at each day with the expectation, understanding, purpose, and pleasure that Jesus wanted for every disciple.

Join me on this joyful, life-changing journey today.

—*Bruce Wilkinson*

Introduction

THE BIG PICTURE
OF YOUR ETERNITY

"Eye has not seen, nor ear heard,
Nor have entered into the heart of man
The things which God has prepared
for those who love Him."

1 CORINTHIANS 2:9

A WELCOME JOLT

"When you give a feast, invite the poor, the maimed, the lame, the blind. And you will be blessed, because they cannot repay you; for you shall be repaid at the resurrection of the just."

LUKE 14:13–14

The woman on talk radio was remembering the night of the 1994 Northridge earthquake in Southern California. Her name was Michelle. When the pictures on the walls of her apartment started falling, and the furniture skidded across the room, and her dishes crashed to the floor, she ran out into the street.

But the earthquake had knocked out the electricity for miles around. Michelle stood unsteadily in a darkened world, wondering what to do.

"By chance I happened to look up," she said. "For the first time in my forty years, I was blessed by the sight of the Milky Way visible above my city. In the midst of so much destruction, it was a glorious sight."

What I want to show you in this book is a big truth that's always been there. But it may have been hidden from you, perhaps for most of your life.

In fact, you may be making critical decisions today as if an immense other reality is not really there at all.

How long can you and I live with a great spiritual truth right in front of us without ever seeing it? A few wrong assumptions can block our view for years.

Until one day we feel a jolt.

That's what it felt like the first time I really heard what Jesus said about the connection between what I do today and what will happen to me in heaven. He said it for the first time during His first recorded public teaching, which we call the Sermon on the Mount:

> "Blessed are you when men hate you,
>> And when they exclude you,
> And revile you, and cast out your name as evil,
>> For the Son of Man's sake.
> Rejoice in that day and leap for joy!
>> For indeed your reward is great in heaven."
>
> LUKE 6:22–23

In other words, suffer for Jesus on earth and He will reward you in heaven. And His reward for you in heaven will be so amazingly wonderful that *if you saw your future like He sees your future…*you would literally leap for joy.

All through the Gospels, Jesus repeatedly connected today with eternity. Take a conversation during a by-invitation-only dinner in His honor at the home of a religious leader. Here's what Jesus told His startled host:

"When you give a feast, invite the poor, the maimed, the lame, the blind. And you will be blessed, because they cannot repay you; for you shall be repaid at the resurrection of the just."

LUKE 14:13–14

Think about your day yesterday. Did you build your priorities around the truth of repayment at the resurrection? Or were you, like so many well-intentioned believers I know, operating on the assumption that *work for God now equals compensation from God now?*

If so, you are seeing only the glare of the temporary where Jesus hopes you'll see the galaxies of eternity. A more accurate equation would be: *More work for God on earth equals more reward from God in heaven.*

Remember when your next-door neighbor was sick and you took dinner over? Hard to believe, but you have a reward coming for that act of service.

Remember when you took a stand at work when everybody else was practicing corruption and you were the only one who didn't? It's time to celebrate, because your stand for Jesus in the face of persecution will bring you great reward.

Today is a day of new beginnings. You are on the brink of a new understanding of the depth of God's love, the expanse of His generosity, and the wonder of His eternal plan…for you.

Ask Jesus to show you that today. Sure, when you first discover what He revealed about eternal rewards, your world may begin to shake. Comfortable assumptions and long-held beliefs start to rattle in the cupboards. But just let the dishes drop. Run out into the street and look up.

Your God is a rewarder.

MY REWARDS JOURNAL: *How does what Jesus revealed about the connection between today and eternity match up (or not match up) with what I assumed or have been taught up to now? How does the truth change my thinking about God? About heaven? About what I want to do today?*

❧

What we need is a big picture of a great God who is utterly committed to joyfully demonstrating his greatness in doing us good. That is, we need to see the majesty of God and know the splendor of God overflowing toward us with exuberant omnipotence. It is not enough to believe that God is big and strong and fearsome—which he is. We must experience this magnificence as the explosion of God's uncontainable zeal to satisfy his creatures by showing them himself.

JOHN PIPER

Two Keys *That* Unlock Forever

For by grace you have been saved through faith, and that not of yourselves;
it is the gift of God, not of works, lest anyone should boast. For we are His
workmanship, created in Christ Jesus for good works, which God prepared
beforehand that we should walk in them.

Ephesians 2:8–10

Remember the first time you learned the truth about the see-saw on the playground? One day your friend jumped off his side without warning—and your side slammed to the ground with a painful *whack!* You'd just received your first lesson on the importance of balance.

What I want to talk to you about today is the critical balance of faith and works. Perhaps you were taught that all the weight should stay on the side of faith. Maybe you grew up suspicious of people who emphasized good works. And by default you decided not only that God doesn't care much about our works on earth, but also that He won't hold us accountable for them in heaven.

Unfortunately, this kind of thinking is off balance. True, Jesus teaches that we are not saved by our works. And what an amazing and precious truth that is! In the text for today, Paul wrote about *our faith:* "For by grace you have been saved through faith, and that not of yourselves; it is the gift of God, not of works, lest anyone should boast" (vv. 8–9).

But notice what Paul said next about *our work.* Though we aren't saved by our works, you and I have been created, saved, and set apart specifically "for good works":

> "For we are His workmanship, created in Christ Jesus for good works, which God prepared beforehand that we should walk in them."

> V. 10

Paul wanted to make it abundantly clear that both works and faith have their places, and both carry great weight when it comes to God's plan for our lives.

In fact, together faith and works unlock our eternal future. In *A Life God Rewards,* I describe these two truths as keys. The first key is your belief, or your faith. The second key is your behavior, or your works.

What you believe about Jesus determines where you will spend eternity—in heaven or in hell. It decides your eternal destination. Jesus said, "He who believes in the Son has everlasting life" (John 3:36).

How you behave on earth determines how God will reward you

in heaven. Your works decide your eternal compensation (or reward). Jesus said, "Behold, I am coming quickly, and My reward is with Me, to give to every one according to his work" (Revelation 22:12).

Compare what these truths mean today for you and everyone you know:

	THE KEY OF BELIEF (FAITH)	THE KEY OF BEHAVIOR (WORKS)
What I Do	I believe in Christ	I work for Christ
What I Receive	Gift from God	Rewards from God
Who Did the Work	Christ did the work for me	I do the work for Christ
The Basis	My faith in Christ	My good works
The Result	My eternal salvation	My eternal compensation
The Amount	All of salvation	As much as I earned
The Comparison	Salvation is the same for everyone because it is a gift	Rewards are different for everyone because they are wages

I hope the whole message of the gospel is coming alive for you in a fresh way today. May the light of its truth rid your mind and heart of these two dangerous misconceptions:

1. *The misconception that your works can lead to salvation.* Never again confuse God's reward for your work with His gift of salvation. Whenever the Bible talks about belief, it cannot have anything to do with rewards. And the reverse is also true: Whenever the Bible talks about works, it cannot have anything to do with salvation.

2. *The misconception that your works don't matter.* Never again say, "It's only what I believe that matters. My works don't matter to God." Your works for God matter greatly to Him—and to you!

As you let Jesus' teachings on salvation and reward change how you think, you'll experience dramatic and positive changes in how you view the opportunities God gives you each day. You'll become convinced that there's a lot more to your life now than just what you believe, and a lot more to your future in heaven than just getting in.

MY REWARDS JOURNAL: *When it comes to what I believe about God's plan for my life, how have my beliefs been out of balance? How will getting them back in balance change my life?*

⟨∞⟩

For a man cannot profit God....
But though we are unprofitable to him,
our serving him is not unprofitable to us.
JOHN WESLEY

Forever *in* Focus

"For the Son of Man will come in the glory of His Father with His angels,
and then He will reward each according to his works."

Matthew 16:27

What will happen when we die? Let's face it, most of us tend
to think of our lives in three stages:

- Stage One: You live on earth. A lot of things happen.
- Stage Two: You die. One thing happens.
- Stage Three: You exist in eternity. Not much ever happens.

But Jesus came to tell us something very different. He revealed
that, actually, almost all of our life happens *after* our physical death.
One day Jesus told His disciples about several important events that
will happen in everyone's future. We see it in today's text:

> "For the Son of Man will come in the glory of His Father
> with His angels, and then He will reward each according to
> his works."
>
> Matthew 16:27

Do you see what Jesus is saying in this verse? At some time in the future, Jesus will return. He will reward—or not reward—everyone. And His rewards will be based on each one's works. That's a lot of activity happening *after* the event of our physical death. And as you're about to see, that's just the beginning.

In fact, since Jesus hasn't yet come again, we know that His disciples are still waiting in heaven for the event that Jesus described in this verse to take place.

In the coming days in this devotional, you'll see how God wants your life today to flourish and count for eternity in ways you never thought possible. But nobody can live enthusiastically for eternity if they don't have a clear idea of how real, important, and eventful our life there will be.

So today let's bring our lives forever into focus with a review of the (real) timeline of our lives. Jesus reveals at least six main events that will take place for every person.

THE SIX MAIN EVENTS OF YOUR FOREVER LIFE

1. Life. *You are created in the image of God for a life of purpose.* Between birth and death, you live on earth as a body, soul, and spirit (John 3:6; 4:23–24; 1 Thessalonians 5:23).
2. Death. *You die physically, but not spiritually.* When you die, your body returns to dust. But you are more than organic matter, and Jesus talked often about the eternal existence of every person (Luke 23:43).

3. Destination. *You reach your destination after death, which is determined by what you believed on earth about Jesus.* Jesus identified only two possible locations in the afterlife: heaven or hell (John 3:16–18; 14:2; Matthew 23:33).

4. Resurrection. *You receive a resurrected body.* Our new bodies will be immortal—they can never again experience death (John 5:28–29; see also 1 Corinthians 15; Philippians 3:21).

5. Repayment. *You receive your reward or your retribution for eternity based on what you did on earth.* Believers and nonbelievers will be judged by Jesus Christ at events called the bema and the great white throne. This judgment will determine the degree of reward in heaven or retribution in hell (John 5:22; 2 Corinthians 5:10; Revelation 20:11–15; Matthew 11:21–22; 23:14).

6. Eternity. You will live forever in the presence or absence of God, reaping the consequences of your beliefs and actions on earth (Matthew 25:46).

Put these six main events in a line; then ask which one event determines everything that follows? Clearly, the single event of your life determines everything about eternity.

In *A Life God Rewards,* I suggested that you picture the timeline like this:[1]

LIFE   EVERY EVENT IN YOUR ETERNITY

The dot represents your life on earth. The line represents eternity and all the events that Jesus revealed will take place there. This illustration shows the relationship of cause and consequence that exists between actions in the dot (your life) and consequences in the line (your eternity).

In other words, everything that happens on the dot—your life of approximately seventy years—determines everything about your eternity!

Have you ever thought about your life on earth that way before? It's startling, isn't it? That's because the truth that we will live forever gets lost in the blinding reality of the here and now. And we have a personal enemy in Satan who likes it that way!

Today I invite you to let the truth of this picture become deeply imprinted on your mind and heart. One day you will give an account to the One who loves you most of what you did in your "dot." And what happens next will change your life—and keep on changing it forever.

MY REWARDS JOURNAL: *How would I live today if it were my last chance to live for the line, not the dot? In light of the big picture of eternity, what changes do I want to make this week in my priorities?*

❧

Do not be deceived, God is not mocked;
for whatever a man sows, that he will also reap.
For he who sows to his flesh will of the flesh reap corruption,
but he who sows to the Spirit will of the Spirit reap everlasting life.
And let us not grow weary while doing good,
for in due season we shall reap if we do not lose heart.

GALATIANS 6:7–9

Week One

❀

THE PROMISE
OF REWARD

*The rewards are such as should make us
leap to think on, and that we should
remember with exceeding joy,
and never think that it is contrary to the
Christian faith to rejoice and be glad for them.*

JOHN BUNYAN, *PILGRIM'S PROGRESS*

THE MISTHOS *of* JESUS

"Everyone who has left houses or brothers or sisters or father or mother or wife or children or lands, for My name's sake, shall receive a hundredfold."
MATTHEW 19:29

O nce when I presented the biblical teachings on rewards at a conference for business executives, I came ready with a stack of hundred-dollar bills.

"I'm considering making you an unusual offer," I said, plunking the bills on the podium in front of me. "If you walk around the outside of this room, I'll give each of you a hundred-dollar bill every time you walk past the podium. You can take a restroom break, but if you leave for any other reason, the deal is off. Otherwise, as long as you keep going around the room, I'll pay up."

Pointing to my briefcase, I said, "By the way, you should assume there's a million dollars in here. So you don't have to worry about me running out."

I asked how many were ready to start walking. Everybody laughed, and a couple presidents and corporate directors jumped to their feet. We all agreed that we had a very motivating proposition on the table.

"If the deal were for real," I asked, "how many in the group would keep walking for a long time?" More laughter. People started making claims about how many hours and days they could stagger on if I kept my promise.

Then I asked, "And how many of you would be saying to yourself while you walked—even when you reached the point of exhaustion—'Oh, man! This is such a sacrifice!'?"

The room quieted. When I asked what my proposal might illustrate regarding the truth of eternal rewards, a woman said, "If God pays us so generously for what we do for Him, then it's not sacrifice, is it?"

She hit the nail on the head. Yes, in this life God asks for our all—our attention, our loyalty, our effort, our time. But in exchange He guarantees to repay us personally, generously, and forever.

We often think of God as our creator, protector, provider, and Savior. But God as employer? Paymaster? Sounds surprising, doesn't it? Yet Jesus described the reward He gives as actual payment.

The first word Jesus used for reward is found in the Sermon on the Mount. In Greek, it is *misthos,* meaning wages.

> "Rejoice in that day and leap for joy! For indeed your *misthos* [wages] are great in heaven."
>
> Luke 6:23

Today, hear these words in Luke as the Boss of heaven saying to you, "If you join My work team, I want you to know something—when you see Me, I will give you your wages."

The second word Jesus used for reward in heaven is a compound word, *apodidomai*. *Apo* means *back*, and *didomai* means *to give*. Combined, *apodidomai* means to give back in return:

> "You will be blessed...for you shall be *apodidomai* [given back in return] at the resurrection of the just."
>
> Luke 14:14

Jesus says that when you receive an *apodidomai*, you are getting back what someone owes you in return for something you gave them.

Jesus has called you to serve in God's kingdom because what you can only guess at, *He knows*...

He knows eternity firsthand.

He knows the full intended purpose of your unique life and circumstances.

He knows that He is storing up reward for you for every genuine work you do for Him—whether a small kindness to a stranger or your lifeblood in martyrdom.

He knows that His plan to reward you—once you realize it in heaven—will make you leap for joy and will forever wipe away any memory of perceived sacrifice.

And He knows that your only regret before Him will be that you didn't serve Him more. And longer. And more truly. And with greater, more joyful anticipation.

Because Jesus came to earth to tell us what He knows about our future, the most important question you and I could ask about the day ahead is, *How do I want to invest the next twelve hours to maximize the rewards Christ will give?*

MY REWARDS JOURNAL: *"Dear Lord, never again will I think of what I do for You as some great sacrifice on my part. From now on..."*

∞

And may the Lord make you increase and abound in love to one another and to all, just as we do to you, so that He may establish your hearts blameless in holiness before our God and Father at the coming of our Lord Jesus Christ with all His saints.

1 THESSALONIANS 3:12–13

DON'T LOOK NOW

By faith Moses, when he became of age, refused to be called the son of Pharaoh's daughter, choosing rather to suffer affliction with the people of God than to enjoy the passing pleasures of sin, esteeming the reproach of Christ greater riches than the treasures in Egypt; for he looked to the reward.

HEBREWS 11:24–26

Recently I spoke for a week to a gathering of 3500 pastors and church leaders in Africa. They loved God and served Him faithfully, but I became aware that they were suffering from a very unfortunate misunderstanding. I wonder if you might be too.

Call it a mistake of timing. Nearly every one of them expected God to reward their service of Him with health and wealth *here on earth.*

"If what you believe is true," I said, probing gently, "then there should be proof because God always keeps His word. Doesn't He?"

Everywhere, heads nodded.

"So, then, how many of you have given sacrificially to God numerous times in your life? Please raise your hand."

Hands shot up all around the room.

Then I asked the difficult question: "How many of you have

become rich, as you believe the Bible teaches? Please raise your hand."

Only one hand out of 3500 went up.

Shock waves reverberated through the crowd, but an enlightening—and ultimately liberating—discussion followed. Here's one of the most painful revelations that came to light: *Everyone in that group privately thought that they were the only person God was not making wealthy and that God was responding this way because of some deep failing on their part!* You can imagine the doubt and discouragement these pastors faced as a result of their wrong belief.

The eternal rewards Jesus spoke about do not come now, but later, in heaven. Yes, godly living will bring you enormous benefit because you are building your life on wisdom and truth. Yes, God answers prayer. And yes, God *may* reward you abundantly in this life for serving Him. He rewards us "in this time" and "in the age to come" (Mark 10:30).

However, His greatest reward by far for what we do—the reward that Jesus, as well as the New Testament writers, spoke about most, and the one that should radically alter our priorities now—comes to us when it will matter *most*—in heaven.

Yet how often we measure God's faithfulness and generosity to us by what is happening now! And how often we hear pastors or media preachers teach that God will always reward or bless us for doing the right thing *in the here and now.*

You will experience new freedom and confidence the minute you receive the truth Jesus brought.

Moses believed in God's future reward, and as Israel's first national leader his belief changed the course of history. In Hebrews 11, we're told that he refused the honor of a royal future in Pharaoh's court, "esteeming the reproach of Christ greater riches than the treasures in Egypt; *for he looked to the reward*" (v. 26). Faith that God would keep His word sustained Moses in the desert through forty years of rebellion, danger, and attack.

Believing in Christ for both our salvation and reward requires faith, doesn't it? Yet when you think about it, everyday life requires faith. We live by faith when we go to work for weeks before being paid. We live by faith when we plan to retire on the earnings of an investment, or when we put in hours of training so we can compete in an athletic event. (I like the T-shirt I saw at the fitness club: "Work hard now. Play hard later.")

Yet as followers of Jesus we can easily lose track of the same truth as it relates to eternity. If we don't see justice or benefit in the here and now, we begin to doubt God's faithfulness. We may even decide not to bother doing the work He's given us to do.

That's why earlier in the same chapter on Moses' example, the Bible says, "Without faith it is impossible to please Him, for he who comes to God must believe that He is, and that He is a rewarder of those who diligently seek Him" (v. 6). Are you questioning God's goodness today? His faithfulness? His favor on your life? Maybe you simply need to resolve the issue of the *timing* of God's reward.

He asks each of us to work hard for Him now, looking not at our circumstances as proof of God's character or guarantee, but to the amazing future He has promised.

MY REWARDS JOURNAL: *Have I misunderstood the timing of God's reward for my good works? How might new and greater faith in His faithfulness change the way I live today?*

For you have need of endurance,
so that after you have done the will of God,
you may receive the promise:
"For yet a little while, and He who is coming
will come and will not tarry.
Now the just shall live by faith."

HEBREWS 10:36–38

The Scripture is full, from beginning to end,
of the proposals of reward.
And the greatest characters have acted on this expectation.

JOSIAH PRATT

Working *in the* Son

"If anyone serves Me, let him follow Me; and where I am, there My servant will be also. If anyone serves Me, him My Father will honor."
John 12:26

I had dinner recently with two men both worth well over $100 million. Howard and Karl are good men, long-time followers of Jesus, and generous and involved citizens. Their enterprises touch millions of lives and impact the economies of nations around the world. But I suspected that they hadn't given much thought to the idea of eternal rewards. I decided to take an approach they might understand.

I proceeded cautiously. "I suppose your people know what their paycheck is going to be at the end of the month. I mean, they don't expect their boss to just pick a number out of a hat." They laughed.

I continued, "And I suppose you have some kind of regular performance review for all your employees. Or do you just do it for some of them?"

All of them, they told me, even senior vice presidents.

I pressed on. "Do you reward these people based on how well they do whatever catches their attention, or on how well they do what they've been hired to do?"

Howard and Karl knew I was up to something, but they decided to humor me. "Only on how well they do what we hired them to do," Karl offered.

Then I asked, "So when you evaluate an employee's overall success, do you measure good intentions or do you measure results?"

"We measure results," they said in unison.

"Why wouldn't God do that too, with us?" I asked. "In fact, if He is wise and good, why wouldn't He do everything we've been talking about?"

The men sat thinking. Finally Howard said, "I have always believed that all God expects of me is to believe in Jesus and try to live a good life. After that—leave the results up to Him." He hesitated. "But you know, I certainly don't run my corporations that way."

What kind of boss is God, anyway? And what is it He wants us, His "employees," to accomplish?

The truth is, most Christians I know—even those who have been going to church all their lives—don't have any more clarity on how God "does business" than Howard and Karl did.

Are you uncomfortable thinking about your spiritual purpose in business terms. Even though it's not the entire picture of how He relates to us, the idea of God as our employer is both useful and true. In fact, Jesus repeatedly told stories about servants (employees) and their masters (bosses) to explain what He expects from us.

God, our "employer," is responsible for an enterprise that would make Howard's and Karl's look like a lemonade stand. He has a clear purpose in mind. And every page of the Bible demonstrates how highly motivated He is to see it accomplished.

And what does God want?

God wants the whole world. He chose to give up His only Son's life for it. He wants to touch every corner of the world and every person in it with His promise of new life. He invites you and me to be an integral part of this mission. He will bring each of us to a day of accounting and reward. And He guarantees that His reward for our service to Him will bless us for all eternity.

Consider: When Jesus promised His friends a hundredfold return on their investment for Him, what was He about to ask of them? The answer is...*everything.*

Peter had just told Jesus, "See, we have left all and followed You" (Matthew 19:27). Would they face trials, opposition, persecution, and even death in the process? Almost certainly. Did He want them to doubt that such a significant life calling was worth it? Not for a moment.

If you know Jesus Christ as your personal Savior, then He asks you to give over your entire life to do His work, and to *know* that it's worth it. We have been invited to serve Him with all of our heart, soul, mind, and might to achieve what He wants.

And He still wants the whole world.

My Rewards Journal: *"Dear Lord, forgive me for failing to understand that You 'hired' me for a reason—and that I'm accountable to You. Today I will…"*

*The most important thought I ever had
was that of my individual responsibility to God.*

Daniel Webster

*"Go therefore and make disciples of all the nations,
baptizing them in the name of the Father and of the Son
and of the Holy Spirit, teaching them to observe
all things that I have commanded you;
and lo, I am with you always, even to the end of the age."*

Matthew 28:19–20

Rug Money

And let our people also learn to maintain good works, to meet urgent needs, that they may not be unfruitful.

Titus 3:14

I t was early in our marriage, and Darlene Marie and I had been putting away money in our "dream jar" for months. Our dream was to buy a rug to put over the cold, hard floor of our tiny house.

One day some missionaries came to stay for the weekend. They had been overseas for years working with the poor and were in town for some speaking engagements. As they were unpacking, Darlene Marie and I noticed the alarmingly sad state of the clothes they were planning to wear.

Our eyes met across the room. We were both thinking, *They can't wear that.* But they had no money, and we had no money…except what was in our dream jar.

After Darlene Marie and I went into our bedroom, we were both quiet. We didn't want to lose our rug money, yet we wanted to buy them clothes. And we sensed what Jesus wanted us to do. Thankfully we made the right decision.

You should have seen the missionaries Sunday morning, radiant in their new attire! That rug money was generating a lot more warmth in their lives than it would have on our floor. Even though we rattled around on cold floors for many more months, my wife and I never regretted our decision for a minute.

When people ask me, "So what is a work that God will reward?" I often think about when we gave away our rug money. My wife and I didn't yet know about Jesus' promise to reward, but we instinctively *knew* that that was what God wanted from us and that our obedience would please Him.

For most of us, simply doing what we know God wants us to do today will lead us to a life He rewards in eternity. I've noticed that nearly everyone knows what a good work for God looks like, even if they don't know about His plan to reward them.

Today's verse describes a good work as meeting "urgent needs." The Bible gives many examples of this: feeding the hungry; working for peace and justice; taking in strangers; caring for the ill, the weak, the abandoned, widows and orphans, and the poor. We're also encouraged to accomplish important spiritual works like spreading the gospel (Acts 10:42), making disciples (Matthew 28:19), bearing each other's burdens (Galatians 6:2), praying for those in authority (1 Timothy 2:1–2), and supporting the work of ministry (2 Corinthians 9:12–13).

A good work is something you do for the right reasons that furthers God's kingdom and brings Him glory. And whenever we set about to do what God wants done, we put ourselves in the center of His will. That is where we experience His greatest power and pleasure, and our own greatest fulfillment. And that is where He promises us the greatest reward later.

But a good work that God will reward is more than a good intention, a kind thought, or an enjoyable spiritual emotion. Let's admit how easily we can confuse nice feelings during a Sunday morning worship service with good works. Or racking up hours at church or in the community because it makes you feel good or you enjoy the admiration of others.

Maybe that's why Paul encouraged the Galatians, "Let each one examine his own work" (Galatians 6:4). We need to live wisely, making sure that, like Jesus, we are always tending to our Father's business with our Father's heart (John 5:17).

Never doubt that God has a challenging and important plan for you to serve Him with your resources and your opportunities. For you, it may not be what's in your dream jar.

But in my experience, you will really start to do—and enjoy—the work of the kingdom when you see an urgent need and then decide to meet it with the very thing you hold most closely.

MY REWARDS JOURNAL: *What urgent needs of others can I identify in somebody's life today? How might I be part of meeting those needs?*

⌒⌒⌒

Man has two great spiritual needs.
One is for forgiveness. The other is for goodness.
BILLY GRAHAM

His Work *and* Yours

Jesus said to them, "My food is to do the will of Him who sent Me, and to finish His work."

John 4:34

Have you ever noticed how enthusiastic Jesus was about His work for God? When He was only twelve, Jesus told Mary and Joseph, "Did you not know that I must be about My Father's business?" (Luke 2:49). At the outset of His public ministry, Jesus gave His job description in one sentence: "My food is to do the will of Him who sent Me, and to finish His work" (John 4:34).

And at the end of His life, He prayed, "I have glorified You on the earth. I have finished the work which You have given Me to do" (John 17:4). Jesus' work of purchasing our redemption was completed at the Cross—that is why He could cry, "It is finished!" (John 19:30).

You see, there is absolutely nothing we can do to help or add to the work Jesus accomplished on the cross. Yet we can't accomplish *our* work without His help! In nearly the same breath Jesus told His disciples He wanted "much fruit," He warned them, "without Me you can do nothing" (John 15:5).

So even though we do the work, God's power is at the source of every good work we produce—or its value is "nothing." That's why Jesus revealed that the secret to the most fruitful life possible is abiding in Him: "I am the vine, you are the branches. He who abides in Me, and I in him, bears much fruit" (John 15:5). That means only by remaining in close relationship with Jesus can we do works for Him that earn rewards in heaven.

Paul painted an amazing picture of this truth for the Corinthians: "God is able to make *all grace* abound toward you, that you, always having *all sufficiency* in *all things*, may have an *abundance for every good work*" (2 Corinthians 9:8–9).

What a picture of God's generosity and love. He makes it possible for us to do good works, and then, even though we could never serve Him enough to pay back His love, He chooses to reward us for working for Him!

As you can see by the chart below, both the gift of our salvation and the reward for our good works are expressions of God's grace. Both the gift and the reward are undeserved. Both originate in the generous heart and will of God.

SALVATION	REWARD
Christ did the work *for me.*	*I* did the work *for Christ.*
Happens at a judgment immediately when I die.	Happens at a judgment later in eternity.
Has to do with *location*—where I end up—heaven or hell.	Has to do with my *compensation* there *(reward* or *retribution).*
Determined by my belief in Jesus before I die.	Determined by my behavior (what I do for God) before I die.
Happens because of God's grace and goodness.	Happens because of God's grace and goodness.

Considering the matchless gift God gave to secure our salvation—the life of His only Son—it shouldn't surprise us that He chooses to reward the work you and I do for our Savior!

As you go about your day today, remember God's surpassing love for you. To open the door of eternity for you, He gave you the unmerited blessing of salvation, and He gives you the unmerited blessing of eternal reward.

You have God's power available to accomplish great things for Him. What could you do that would show Him how much you value His gifts?

MY REWARDS JOURNAL: *How much have I been relying on God's power to accomplish His work? How might abiding—spending more time in His presence—help equip me for "every good work"?*

*Saint Augustine said that it's only by the grace of God that
we ever do anything even approximating a good work,
and none of our works are worthy enough to
demand that God reward them.
The fact that God has decided to grant rewards
on the basis of obedience or disobedience is what Augustine
called God's crowning of His own work within us.*

R. C. SPROUL

WHO ATE MY CHEESECAKE?

Now he who plants and he who waters are one, and each one will receive his own reward according to his own labor.

1 CORINTHIANS 3:8

How are you feeling by now about living for eternal reward? Once most people get over the surprise of discovering what Jesus said about it, they usually arrive at the obstacle of motivation. *But I was happy serving God because I love Him,* they're likely to think. *I don't need or want reward.*

One woman told me, "I feel unspiritual every time you say the word *reward!*"

Can you relate to her strong feelings? If so, I want to encourage you today. The fact that you're struggling with your motivation for following Jesus says good things about you! You want to do the right thing for the right reasons. You care about genuineness and integrity in your relationship with God. You are wisely cautious about anything that smacks of selfishness or acquisitiveness.

Is it selfish to want God's reward?

The truth is, God created us as complex beings who choose how to act for many reasons. Too often people confuse the idea of mixed motives with multiple motives. *Mixed motives* means that both good and bad intentions are causing our behavior. But *multiple motives* simply means we're doing something for more than one good reason. And, in fact, we usually have more than one good motive when we do anything.

In one brief passage in 2 Corinthians 5, we see that Paul was motivated in three biblical ways—including the hope of reward:

1.   The hope of reward: "We make it our aim…to be well pleasing to Him. For we must all appear before the judgment seat of Christ, that each one may receive…" (vv. 9–10).

2.   The fear of the Lord and an awareness of accountability before Christ: "Knowing, therefore, the terror of the Lord, we persuade men…" (v. 11).

3.   The love of God: "The love of Christ compels us…" (v. 14).

All these motivations came together for Paul, giving him a singular and powerful focus to serve God. Were Paul's motivations selfish just because he knew that he would be rewarded? Not at all.

As you measure your own heart and mind today in light of God's will for you, consider some reasons that you too can be purely motivated for eternal reward:

- *Because eternal reward is God's idea, not ours.* If you decided to offer to pay your son for a task, would you be offended if your offer motivated him? Would you berate him when he came to collect by saying, "I can't believe you actually expect me to pay you"? Of course not.

- *Because the only way to earn eternal reward is to be selfless.* By definition, any good work for God cannot be a selfish act. Jesus said that the Pharisees would not be rewarded because their motive was wrong (Matthew 23:14). God never rewards selfishness, only selflessness.

- *Because eternal rewards are individual and unlimited.* An act is selfish only if you put yourself before others, or prevent others from a getting a share of what you have—for example, if you eat the last piece of cheesecake, knowing that your spouse wanted it. But God rewards each of us personally and out of His limitless bounty. When you receive a reward from Him, no one else is losing what would be rightfully theirs.

- *Because God has a right to do what He wants with what is His.* Jesus revealed God's perspective on repayment in the Parable of the Laborers. When workers questioned the landowner's wage policy, he said, "Is it not lawful for me to do what I wish with my own things? Or is your eye evil because I am good?" (Matthew 20:15).

- *Because it is impossible for God to tempt us!* Any motivation from God is pure and without manipulation (James 1:13). And God said we *must* believe and act in faith on the fact that He is a rewarder (Hebrews 11:6).

Dear friend, please don't leave this chapter thinking that eternal rewards are merely part of a bonus plan for a few ambitious Christians. Eternal rewards are God's idea and His revealed truth; therefore we can never decide that to live for His reward is selfish or even optional.

I promise that in the days ahead we'll look carefully at each question and reservation you might have until a new and remarkably larger view of God's plan for your life shines through.

MY REWARDS JOURNAL: *What are three good things I've done in the last week? What multiple good motives did I have? How did they help me accomplish what I did?*

If we consider the unblushing promises of reward
and the staggering nature of the rewards promised in the Gospels,
it would seem that Our Lord finds our desires
not too strong, but too weak.

C. S. LEWIS

In Your presence is fullness of joy;
At Your right hand are pleasures forevermore.

PSALM 16:11

WASTE NO TIME

See then that you walk circumspectly, not as fools but as wise, redeeming the time, because the days are evil. Therefore do not be unwise, but understand what the will of the Lord is.

EPHESIANS 5:15–17

After Michelangelo died, someone found in his studio a piece of paper on which he had written a note to his apprentice. It read: "Draw, Antonio, draw, Antonio, draw and do not waste time."

The great artist knew that time was both friend and foe to anyone who endeavored to accomplish much in his lifetime. If the goal was worthy, not even an hour was to be wasted.

In the same way, our opportunity to work for God and earn reward has a time limitation. It ends with our last heartbeat. But the impact of what we do for God, since it will last throughout eternity, is nearly infinite. No wonder Paul urged his readers more than once to redeem the time (Ephesians 5:16; Colossians 4:5).

Time spent pursuing good achievements—even noble ones—if not done for God will ultimately be wasted. But time redeemed for Him is time rewarded by Him.

Remember, God isn't looking for supersaints, or for the famous.

He's looking for *you*. There are people only you can touch, places only you can go, words only you can speak. God wants to use you not *in spite of* your circumstances, but precisely *because of* them. Every person on earth has an equal amount of hours in the day—and can find creative ways to "redeem" them for God.

Are you a mom at home with young children and a new baby? No one understands the extent of your service more than God does. He sees every sacrifice, every diaper change, every prayer in the night over a sick child.

Are you a college student attending school far from home? Every time you choose not to cheat, God notices. Every time you stand up for your faith in the face of opposition, God says, "Leap for joy!" (Luke 6:23).

Are you a businessperson, truck driver, or clerk? God has appointments in mind for you today, and the consequences of these appointments will matter to you and others far into the future.

As you read this little book, you might be considering radically redirecting your life to live for God's reward, yet feel that the odds are stacked against you. You might feel discouraged as you compare yourself to others who haven't made the same mistakes. You might feel that your opportunity to do something for God is severely limited by ability, age, or even where you live.

But the value of our work for God, Paul wrote, is "according to what one has, and not according to what he does not have" (2 Corinthians 8:12). In the Parable of the Talents, Jesus made it clear that our Master judges us on what we do with what we have been given (Matthew 25:14–30).

God is ready today to complete the good work He has begun in you (Philippians 1:6). Look around you and notice the people and needs that make up your world. In *The Prayer of Jabez* we called this your "territory." It belongs to you and you alone for a very big reason. It is your opportunity to change your world for God and change your eternity, by His grace, for yourself.

Work. Love. Pray. Give. Do the good work God has gifted you to do for Him.

And do not waste time.

MY REWARDS JOURNAL: *What three "time wasters" am I involved with that I could replace with a redemptive, rewardable activity?*

❧

Now is a day of change; then is a day of no change.
Now is a day of becoming; then is a day of being what
I have become for all eternity.

DR. EARL RADMACHER

I pray…that you may approve the things that are excellent, that you may be sincere and without offense till the day of Christ, being filled with the fruits of righteousness which are by Jesus Christ, to the glory and praise of God.

PHILIPPIANS 1:9–11

❧

THE GOOD NEWS
OF THE BEMA

*Let all men recollect that their work must be
tried by the fire, and anticipate the decisions
which the day of judgment will pronounce.*

MATTHEW HENRY

THE PERSON *on the* PLATFORM

"For the Father judges no one, but has committed all judgment to the Son, that all should honor the Son just as they honor the Father."

JOHN 5:22–23

At the end of his life, Paul was still straining forward, eagerly anticipating his appearance before Jesus his Judge on "that Day" (2 Timothy 4:8). Martin Luther once said that there were only two days on his calendar—today and "that Day."

What is the day in question? What could be so important and compelling about it for you and me? And if it is an appointment with a judge, why would anyone eagerly look forward to it?

This week we'll look at the startling idea that a day of *judgment* for you and me should actually be one of the most important, hope-filled, and motivating truths in the New Testament.

First, come with me to a field of flowers and stone in southern Greece. Here the hot Mediterranean sun beats down on worn marble slabs and a jumble of broken columns—the ruins of the ancient city of Corinth. As you enter the central square of what used to be the marketplace, you'll notice an imposing marble platform raised above the surrounding area.

Stand there.

The apostle Paul stood in the same spot many centuries ago when he was accused of persuading others to worship God in unlawful ways (Acts 18:13). Scholars believe that the raised marble platform still visible at the ruins of Corinth is the exact place where the magistrate Gallio sat to hear Paul's case. On that occasion, he dismissed all charges against Paul.

The platform was called the *bema,* the Greek word for *judgment seat.* Officials at athletic contests also sat at a bema. To everyone in Jesus' day, the bema represented authority, justice, and reward.

Three years after Paul stood at the bema in Corinth, he sent a letter back to the believers there, urging every Christian to live for God in a particular way—knowing that they would all one day appear before the bema of Christ:

> For we must all appear before the judgment seat (bema) of
> Christ, that each one may receive the things done in the
> body, according to what he has done, whether good or bad.
>
> 2 CORINTHIANS 5:10

Paul was writing about the same day of reckoning and reward that Jesus told His disciples about when He said, "The Son of Man will come...and then He will reward each according to his works" (Matthew 16:27).

I believe a large part of Paul's zeal came from knowing that the results of his life would be evaluated with perfect justice and that he would receive his reward.

But there's more. You see, Paul knew that perfect justice at the bema would come not from some grim tribunal or faceless formula, but from a Person—the Lord of perfect love Himself, Jesus Christ.

Whatever you face today, remember that the Judge of your life is none other than the One who came to earth, experienced your humanity, carried your sorrows, and chose to die for you so that you could have everlasting life. "The Father…has committed all judgment to the Son," Jesus said (John 5:22).

Only when you and I stand before this One, on our day of distribution, will we know the depth and breadth of His amazing compassion and commitment for us. And we will see His joy for each of us when He says, "Well done, good and faithful servant!"

Why can you eagerly anticipate the bema today?

Because of the One you will meet face-to-face there. And because His name is Jesus, you can live today with great hope, in every way making it your aim to be well pleasing to Him.

MY REWARDS JOURNAL: *How does the idea of standing before Jesus at a judgment seat make me feel? How might the knowledge of this appointment change the way I think about my walk with God?*

∽⊗∾

The believer has his foundation in Jesus Christ.
Now we are to build upon this foundation,
and the work we have done must stand the ultimate test;
final exams come at the Judgment Seat of Christ
when we receive our rewards.

BILLY GRAHAM

THE OVERLOOKED
TRUTH *of the* BEMA

We shall all stand before the judgment seat of Christ.

ROMANS 14:10

I t appears that a majority of Christians around the world today
do not know about or live for the Day that both Jesus and Paul
talked about so urgently.

Why? Perhaps some think that only people who rejected Christ
will be judged, not those who accepted Him. Perhaps others think
that because Christians have been saved from sin, we will also be
excused from our life—both its responsibilities and its opportunities.
And many just don't know the facts.

Based on your experience, would you agree or disagree with such
strong statements?

Today I want to give you an overview of the biblical teaching
about the believer's judgment, then show you why the practical
implications of this overlooked truth are so important for your life
and mine.

Paul's teachings (see references that follow) give us a clear picture of what will happen at the bema of Jesus. We examined this carefully in *A Life God Rewards,* but here is a summary chart to help you see the big picture quickly.

THE OVERLOOKED TRUTH OF THE BELIEVER'S JUDGMENT	
What is it called?	The Judgment Seat of Christ (*bema* in Greek)
Who will appear?	Everyone who believes in Jesus and has received His free gift of salvation
Who will be the judge?	Jesus Christ
When will it occur?	At Christ's coming
Where?	In heaven
What will be judged?	Our works for God
How?	Our works will be tested by fire
Why?	So that an eternal reward can be given— or lost—on the basis of the lasting value of our works

(Key texts: Romans 14:9–12; 1 Corinthians 3:12–15; 2 Corinthians 5:8–10)

If this information is new to you, how are you feeling as you process it? Anxious? Hopeful? Alarmed? Two common reactions are: feeling *confirmed* in your belief that your sins won't be judged in heaven, but feeling *surprised* that your works for God will be judged.

Followers of Jesus who do not live with the bema in mind have settled for a dangerous deception—*that there will be no time of accounting and reward in eternity for what they did on earth.*

The consequences of this deception are not hard to spot. Many Christians do not see why they should live each day in every way for God. In fact, numerous recent studies show that there are all too few observable differences between the values and behavior of Christians and those of non-Christians.

By the way, can you think of a deception—apart from a deception about our salvation—that Satan would be more interested in spreading among the followers of Jesus?

Thankfully, the facts of the bema can prepare us for genuine spiritual breakthroughs today.

What the Bema Means for Me Today

What the Bema Reveals about My Life	What the Bema Reveals about God
My works today will be judged…	because God is fair.
My works today will be rewarded…	because God is fair and generous.
My works today may add up to little or nothing (I may "suffer loss")…	because God is fair and impartial.
My life on earth today (what I do for God here) will change my eternity…	because God will reward me in heaven.

As you go about your day, measure how you order your priorities by what you know about the bema. And measure how you think about God by what the bema reveals about Him.

You'll find, as have so many others, that the overlooked news of the bema can liberate you to live like the eternally destined being that you are.

MY REWARDS JOURNAL: *How does the truth of the bema change the way I think about God? How is it promising news to me personally?*

◈

The heavenly Father has no spoiled children.
He loves them all too much to allow that.
FRED MITCHELL

Revealed *by* Fire

Now if anyone builds on this foundation with gold, silver, precious stones, wood, hay, straw, each one's work will become clear; for the Day will declare it, because it will be revealed by fire; and the fire will test each one's work, of what sort it is. If anyone's work which he has built on it endures, he will receive a reward.

1 Corinthians 3:12–14

Amy served God by caring for discarded and abused girls in southern India. Most of them had been abandoned or sold into slavery as temple child prostitutes. Although she was a pale-skinned young Irishwoman, Amy dressed in Indian garb, learned Tamil, and didn't leave India for fifty-seven years. Amy never married, suffered from ill health all of her life, and spent her last twenty years raising funds for her "daughters" from bed.

Her name was Amy Carmichael, and her biographer, Elisabeth Elliot, traces her inspiring life of ministry to a turning point when she was a young girl in Belfast....

One rainy Sunday, Amy was heading home from church in her best clothes when she and her brothers met a ragged old woman carrying a heavy load. Deciding they should help, they took her load and held her up as they walked through the streets.

"This meant facing all the respectable people who were, like ourselves, on their way home. It was a horrid moment," Amy recalled
later. "We were only two boys and a girl, and not at all exalted
Christians. We hated doing it."[2]

As the odd little group passed a fountain, a Scripture flashed into
Amy's mind:

> Now if anyone builds on this foundation with gold, silver,
> precious stones, wood, hay, straw, each one's work will
> become clear; for the Day will declare it, because it will be
> revealed by fire; and the fire will test each one's work, of what
> sort it is. If anyone's work which he has built on it endures,
> he will receive a reward.
>
> 1 CORINTHIANS 3:12–14

Amy turned, certain that someone had spoken the familiar
Scripture to her. But she saw no one—only the fountain, and the
falling rain, and people staring at their little procession.

"The children plodded on," Elliot writes, "but something had
happened to the girl which changed forever her life's values." A life
"revealed by fire" became the measure of what was worth doing for
Amy Carmichael. Not what felt convenient, or respectable, or—at
the moment—rewarding. But what would endure the fire.[3]

The picture of the fire at the bema must have had a powerful
impact on the Christians at Corinth, too. Their city, historians tell us,
had recently been ravaged by a major blaze. They had seen firsthand the
power of fire to test whether a building material would endure or not.

"It is the property of fire to test the qualities of objects," writes one commentator. This helps us to understand an important point about the fire at the bema. Paul is writing about the quality of our works, not the cleansing of our sins. Wood, hay, and straw represent acts that don't appear to be wrong and may even appear desirable and worthy on earth, but will burn up as worthless at the bema.

Consider these criteria for enduring quality in what you do today:

- *Enduring works are done in God's power.* Jesus said, "He who abides in Me, and I in him, bears much fruit; for without Me you can do nothing" (John 15:5).
- *Enduring works are done for God's glory.* Jesus said that those who do good works—such as charitable deeds, prayer, and fasting—for the purpose of impressing others already have their reward (Matthew 6:3–5).
- *Enduring works are done according to God's will.* Jesus said, "I do not seek My own will but the will of the Father who sent Me" (John 5:30).

No matter how worthy the activity you pursue today, if it is not done in God's power and for God's glory and according to God's will, it will burn.

And think about this today: What lasts is nearly always what doesn't come easily. Precious metals and stones are often hidden from view. Only by great effort are they mined, refined, and polished.

In the same way, to render a service to God that will endure the fire requires that you give your life away—whether for one day or for many years. Amy Carmichael often said, "You can give without loving, but you cannot love without giving."

MY REWARDS JOURNAL: *If my appointment at the bema took place in heaven today, how would what I have built with my life withstand the test? And why do I believe this?*

⸎

Let no man flatter himself on the ground that,
in the opinion of men, he is reckoned among the
most eminent master builders,
for as soon as the day breaks in,
his whole work must go utterly for nothing
if it is not approved of by the Lord.
JOHN CALVIN

SIN *at the* BEMA

But this Man, after He had offered one sacrifice for sins forever, sat down at the right hand of God.... For by one offering He has perfected forever those who are being sanctified.... "Their sins and their lawless deeds I will remember no more."

HEBREWS 10:12, 14, 17

The tested-by-fire passage in 1 Corinthians 3 ends with these words: "If anyone's work is burned, he will *suffer loss;* but he himself will be saved, yet so as through fire" (v. 15).

The idea of loss in heaven seems like a contradiction, doesn't it? And to "be saved, yet so as through fire" certainly sounds threatening. Let's spend a few minutes on the important questions this verse raises.

First, as today's text so clearly states, when you come to Christ and accept His sacrifice for your sins, your sin and its penalty pass over to Jesus' account. And since He has paid the price for you with His blood, you are "perfected forever"—free, forgiven, and your sins forgotten.

So you can be confident that you will not be condemned at the bema for your sins.

Paul also makes it clear that your salvation is not at stake at the bema. Why? Because only your works are being judged at the bema, not what you believed about Jesus on earth. A person could leave the bema with few or no rewards, yet he will remain in heaven. That's what Paul means when he writes, "saved, yet so as through fire."

So does this mean that sin won't matter at the bema? Just the opposite! Your sins won't be revisited at the bema, but their consequences will directly affect the rewards you receive.

This is why the apostle John warned, "Look to yourselves, that we do not lose those things we worked for, but that we may receive a full reward" (2 John 1:8). It even seems clear from these passages that you could do a work and then later, because of something you did, miss out on the full reward you had coming.

Here's an example:

You're a successful businessman in Singapore and a high-profile Christian. You lead a Bible study for executives and you are active in civic leadership. But in later life, you become entangled in corruption. Eventually, it comes to light. A well-publicized trial unravels your reputation and sends you to prison. Many who had been influenced to follow Christ by your example turn away, bitter and disillusioned.

When you appear at the bema, will you receive the *full reward* you earned for your years of service? Or will you "suffer loss" because of your actions later in life?

I hope you can see how the consequences of our sins can still cause us to suffer loss at the bema. Anything less than a joyous "Well done!" from our Lord will seem like a waste of a life.

The disciple Peter knew what "suffer loss" felt like. It was the night before Jesus was to be crucified, and He was already under arrest. But waiting at a campfire nearby, Peter denied three times that he followed Jesus or even knew who He was.

Then a cock crowed, as Jesus had predicted. Peter looked up and met Jesus' gaze across the courtyard:

> The Lord turned and looked at Peter. Then Peter remembered
> the word of the Lord.... So Peter went out and wept bitterly.
>
> LUKE 22:61–62

How painful that one glance from his Lord must have been! Not hateful or condemning, but full of the truth of what could have been.

In the same way, when we stand before Jesus at the bema, we will look into His face. Could anything be more painful than to feel shame and regret at that moment?

No wonder John pleaded with believers to live in such a way that shame would be out of the question when we appear before Christ. "And now, little children, abide in Him, that when He appears, we may have confidence and not be ashamed before Him at His coming" (1 John 2:28).

Join me in living wholeheartedly for a day of celebration, not disappointment, at the bema. Nothing we could experience on earth will compare to the prize of seeing joy on Jesus' face as He leans forward to show His gratitude and pleasure.

MY REWARDS JOURNAL: *Have I stopped being grateful for the for-giveness of my sins? Have I stopped making every effort not to sin?*

"Lord, I want to run my race not just to pass the finish, but to finish well!"

> *Payment God cannot twice demand:*
> *first at my bleeding Savior's hand,*
> *and then again at mine.*
>
> AUGUSTUS TOPLADY

> *Therefore we also, since we are surrounded*
> *by so great a cloud of witnesses,*
> *let us lay aside every weight,*
> *and the sin which so easily ensnares us,*
> *and let us run with endurance the race that is set before us.*
>
> HEBREWS 12:1

A HOUSE *on the* ROCK

"Whoever hears these sayings of Mine, and does them, I will liken him to
a wise man who built his house on the rock: and the rain descended, the
floods came, and the winds blew and beat on that house; and it did not
fall, for it was founded on the rock. But everyone who hears these sayings
of Mine, and does not do them, will be like a foolish man who built his
house on the sand: and the rain descended, the floods came, and the winds
blew and beat on that house; and it fell. And great was its fall."

MATTHEW 7:24–27

Not far from where I used to live in Oregon is an island that hides a secret—of a town that fell into the sea.

The island is all that remains of a peninsula that looked like prime real estate in the early part of the twentieth century. Developers laid out the streets for a town and named it Bayocean. Families built homes. A three-story hotel went up on the top of a bluff 140 feet above the ocean. Picnickers from Portland crowded the beaches.

But the town was built on sand, and winter storms started taking their toll. One house at a time, Bayocean tumbled into the waves. By 1952, the town—including the hotel, the bluff, and most of the peninsula—had washed away.

Stories like this one leave us with a hollow feeling, don't they? All that effort for nothing. All those hopes vanishing without a trace.

In today's text, Jesus teaches about the importance of building our life on what will last—through this life and for eternity. After all, before the result of our life can ever be evaluated by Jesus in heaven, it must survive the trials and temptations of this world.

But how do you build a "house" that will survive? Jesus put it in very direct terms. The person whose house rests on rock is "whoever hears these sayings of Mine, and *does them*" (v. 24).

Obedience—doing the truth—may be the most important rule for building a storm-proof life. "The evidence of knowing God is obeying God," writes one commentator. How easy it is for us to listen to Jesus' words, fit them into our beliefs, nod our heads in agreement…and take no action. Yet this response—so recognizable and common—is as dangerous as staking our future on a hill of sand. James wrote, "But be doers of the word, and not hearers only, *deceiving yourselves*" (James 1:22).

Jesus pointed out the importance of doing, not just knowing, the truth in a similar story in Luke's Gospel. In this instance, Jesus used the image of building on a foundation:

> "But why do you call Me 'Lord, Lord,' and not do the things which I say…? But he who heard and did nothing is like a man who built a house on the earth without a foundation, against which the stream beat vehemently; and immediately it fell. And the ruin of that house was great."

6:46, 49

Amazing, isn't it? God's blueprint for a life that endures is simple enough for anyone to understand: Listen to the truth and do it.

Today, I invite you to do a building inspection of your life. Ask yourself, *What did Jesus tell His followers to do?* What comes to mind? I'll get you started:

> *Give…*
>
> *Forgive…*
>
> *Resist temptation…*
>
> *Turn the other cheek…*
>
> *Deny yourself…*
>
> *Love God and love your neighbor as yourself…*
>
> *Go and preach the gospel…*

Place a check mark by the things you have actively been doing the past few weeks. Have you been deceiving yourself, as James warned? Remember, you and I will not be rewarded in heaven for what we heard and believed, only for what we did for God.

How wonderful that you and I don't have to guess what it will take to please God with the building of our life! Today we have the teachings of Jesus, and of the whole Bible, and the guidance of the Holy Spirit. And today we have many more opportunities to obey— and impact eternity.

Within sight of the deserted sands of Bayocean stands a small lighthouse. It's been there through fog, sleet, wind, and darkness for a hundred years, shining a beacon out to sea. Why has the lighthouse endured when the town didn't? Because the lighthouse was built two hundred feet above the waves…and its foundation rests on solid rock.

Make that a picture of what you want your life to be for God. If you are ready to listen *and* do, you can build your life with confidence, certain that when trials and storms come your way, your house will stand and your service to God will shine for all eternity.

MY REWARDS JOURNAL: *"Lord, please reveal to me today what I have been hearing You say again and again in my life but have willfully chosen not to do."*

❦

No other foundation can anyone lay than that which is laid, which is Jesus Christ.

1 CORINTHIANS 3:11

Blessed is the man who endures temptation; for when he has been approved, he will receive the crown of life which the Lord has promised to those who love Him.

JAMES 1:12

Therefore, my dear brothers, stand firm. Let nothing move you. Always give yourselves fully to the work of the Lord, because you know that your labor in the Lord is not in vain.

1 CORINTHIANS 15:58, NIV

THE CROWN LAID UP *for* YOU

Finally, there is laid up for me the crown of righteousness, which the Lord, the righteous Judge, will give to me on that Day, and not to me only but also to all who have loved His appearing.

2 TIMOTHY 4:8

Do you think of heaven as a warm and fuzzy experience where nothing goes wrong...but nothing happens either?

Scripture teaches something quite different—that we will have a full, productive, and meaningful life in heaven. For example, Jesus told His disciples that in the eternal kingdom they would serve, rule, judge, worship, enjoy relationships, fellowship intimately with Him, eat and drink, have responsibility, and enjoy intense pleasures.

That's one reason rewards will matter greatly to you in heaven. They will directly affect how you experience heaven—for example, what you are granted to do there, and how much you are privileged to serve God.

Jesus gave certain rewards more emphasis than others:

- *Authority or rulership.* To His disciples, Jesus promised, "You who have followed Me will also sit on twelve thrones, judging the twelve tribes of Israel" (Matthew 19:28).

- *Honor.* To all of His followers, Jesus said, "If anyone serves Me, him My Father will honor" (John 12:26).

Another specific reward, described in the book of Daniel, applies to everyone who leads others to God:

"Those who are wise shall shine
    Like the brightness of the firmament,
And those who turn many to righteousness
    Like the stars forever and ever."

DANIEL 12:3

Perhaps the most common symbol of reward in the New Testament is a crown. In their culture and in ours, a crown stands for the highest symbol of honor.

Two Greek words lie behind the word translated *crown. Diadema* refers to a regal crown, the badge of royalty. This is the word applied to the crowns Christ himself will wear (Revelation 19:12). The second word is *stephanos,* which designates the wreath, garland, or crown presented to the victor at the public athletic games. It's a symbol of triumph and victory, a token of public honor for distinguished service. These are the crowns that believers will receive for serving God, but represent only a small portion of the eternal rewards the New Testament outlines.

Several crowns are mentioned specifically in the New Testament, but there's no reason to believe that these are to be taken as an exhaustive list:

- *Crown of glory.* Peter encouraged church leaders to "shepherd the flock of God" in such a way that "when the Chief

Shepherd appears, you will receive the crown of glory that does not fade away" (1 Peter 5:1–4).

- *Crown of life.* Those who endure severe temptations, suffering, and tribulation in faithfulness and love will receive a special crown of life. This does not refer to the gift of eternal life, but a reward for good works (James 1:12; Revelation 2:10).

- *Crown of righteousness.* Paul tells Timothy that all who long for the return of the Lord will receive a crown of righteousness. John says that a person who desires Jesus' return "purifies himself, just as He is pure" (2 Timothy 4:6–8; 1 John 3:2–3).

- *Crown of joy.* Paul describes those who have responded to his ministry as his "crown of rejoicing." This indicates a crown for those who have brought others into the kingdom (1 Thessalonians 2:19).

- *Imperishable crown.* Paul compares the Christian life with the Isthmian games, well-known to the Corinthians. Those runners compete "to obtain a perishable crown, but we for an imperishable crown" (1 Corinthians 9:25). Some scholars interpret this to indicate a specific crown for believers who show extraordinary self-control, discipline, self-denial, and single-mindedness in their work for God—the same qualities an athlete needs to win.

Even though the Bible doesn't tell us the exact nature of these crowns, one thing is very clear—He wanted us to know that the rewards are highly desirable. In fact, Jesus wants us to keep our rewards (as opposed to giving them back to Him) because they will change our experience of heaven—and our ability to serve Him—for all eternity.

When you arrive in heaven, what do you want to have accomplished with the singular opportunity and miracle of your life? Paul said, "Do you not know that those who run in a race all run, but one receives the prize? Run in such a way that you may obtain it" (1 Corinthians 9:24).

Let the prize of God's highest honor and praise shape your every choice today.

MY REWARDS JOURNAL: *How do I think I will feel when Jesus hands me my rewards—and wants me to keep them? What rewards do I most want to earn—and what am I doing toward that end?*

"Behold, I am coming quickly!
Hold fast what you have,
that no one may take your crown."
REVELATION 3:11

The Good News *of* Accountability

*In this you greatly rejoice, though now for a little while, if need be, you
have been grieved by various trials, that the genuineness of your faith,
being much more precious than gold that perishes, though it is tested by
fire, may be found to praise, honor, and glory at the revelation of Jesus
Christ.*

1 Peter 1:6–7

The first time I examined what the Bible says about the bema
seat, God's plan didn't seem fair, loving, or even likable. You
may feel the same way right now. Yet because you have a deep desire
to know God's very best for your life (that's why you're reading this
page), I believe that you are ready to receive the extraordinary
promise of accountability at the bema.

I hope you sense a greater awe and reverence for God's tenacious
love for you and also for His important expectations for your life. I
hope you feel a growing motivation to accumulate good works for
God, starting now, that will survive the test of the fire. And I trust
you are experiencing a growing determination to put away the sins

that sabotage your joy now and your potential for even greater joy in heaven.

You see, accountability in a family is good news! It is a memorial stone to commitment, love, justice, and promise. Every time you measure your day by it, you rise a little more to what it truly means to be a child of God.

Think about it: What kind of father would God be if He just granted us blanket forgiveness, then never cared enough about our present or future well-being to check up on us?

The truth is that every child of God longs for accountability. We want to be noticed. We want to matter. Deep down, we know we've been called to accomplish something important and that we won't be satisfied until we do. "Teach us to number our days, that we may gain a heart of wisdom," wrote Moses (Psalm 90:12). The knowledge that God will ask us to account for our gift of days actually helps us seize our best destiny.

Perhaps by now you see what I do—that a passionless, compromised life as a follower of Christ can often be traced directly to a set of terribly misguided assumptions. Something like:

"What I do now only matters now...

And anyway, I'm forgiven...

And besides, no one notices."

But I hope you're putting together a very different picture of the life God wants for you. Think of it as two halves of a circle:

One half says:

"God wants to reward me—and the hope of reward in heaven can change my life today."

The other half says:

"God will hold me accountable—and a godly fear of loss of rewards in heaven can change my life today."

As you bring these two astounding truths together, you will see the larger picture of your life, and you'll be more motivated than ever before to reach for the life God created you for.

MY REWARDS JOURNAL: *"Dear Lord, I am beginning to understand just how good the news of the bema really is! Today show me specific areas where I have made unwise compromises because I misunderstood this issue of accountability…"*

❧

But, beloved, we are confident of better things concerning you,
yes, things that accompany salvation…. For God is not unjust to forget
your work and labor of love which you have shown toward His name,
in that you have ministered to the saints, and do minister.
And we desire that each one of you show the same diligence to the full
assurance of hope until the end, that you do not become sluggish, but
imitate those who through faith and patience inherit the promises.

HEBREWS 6:9–12

Week Three

∞

LIVING THE LIFE
GOD REWARDS

*Therefore, my beloved brethren,
be steadfast, immovable, always abounding
in the work of the Lord, knowing that your
labor is not in vain in the Lord.*

1 CORINTHIANS 15:58

Returns *of the* Day

"A certain nobleman went into a far country to receive for himself a kingdom and to return. So he called ten of his servants, delivered to them ten minas, and said to them, 'Do business till I come.'"

Luke 19:12–13

How do you make a thousand dollars when all you have in your pocket is a quarter?"

I remember posing the question to my wife. We were starting a family and trying to get by on what I earned as a first-year college instructor, which wasn't much. And our resources were dwindling fast.

A few days later, I used that quarter to call my father. I had spotted a run-down house for sale that I thought I could fix up for a profit. Would he lend me the down payment? Dad agreed and sent $3,000.

I got started cleaning the place up right away, but soon I realized I had another problem—I didn't have enough time to remodel and keep up with my teaching. Then I remembered that a builder friend of mine was out of work. So I proposed another deal: If he would provide the skilled labor, I would buy the supplies. When we were done, we could split the profit.

My friend thought it was a great idea. So while I taught, he remodeled. Three months later, I sold the house. After dividing the earnings with my partner, I took home $14,000—more money than my entire year's salary!

My investment of one quarter had yielded a huge return. In business terms, you'd call that leverage—using a little to get back a lot.

In chapters 5 and 6 of *A Life God Rewards,* we looked at how God wants us to impact eternity with our time, talent, and treasure. And we discovered that God actually expects us to take whatever He has placed in our keeping on earth and put it to work for Him for a great return in eternity.

Investment, assets, leverage, return—it's not the usual language of the deeper spiritual life, is it? Yet it is startlingly close to the language Jesus used when He talked about how He wanted His disciples to live for Him on earth.

Today's passage begins Jesus' familiar Parable of the Minas. A nobleman is leaving to receive a kingdom. But he *will* return. In the meantime, he commissions his servants to take what he has placed in their keeping and pursue something very important—"Do business till I come."

When the nobleman returns, only the servant who has grown his asset exponentially—from one mina to ten—receives his lord's highest praise and highest reward. The servant who hid his asset, on the other hand, receives neither praise nor reward. In fact, he loses his one mina to the servant who had earned ten more.

What does Jesus want us to learn about living for eternity from this parable?

- Jesus is purposeful, not casual or indifferent, about our work for Him.
- Jesus gave us our individual abilities, interests, resources, and opportunities for a reason. They may seem small—like a quarter in your pocket—but their potential for eternal return is enormous.
- Jesus expects a *significant* return on His investment.
- Jesus will return for a day of accounting and reward (or loss of reward). What we have done with His asset on earth will determine His response and our potential for further service in heaven.

This week we look at what it means to steward our days for God. We'll talk about serving, sacrificing, submitting—all topics you may be familiar with. But don't miss the big idea: Our soon-returning Lord created us uniquely for today, knows exactly what He has put in our care, sees exactly its eternal potential...*and is expecting a major return!*

Are you willing to begin believing and living toward what God knows to be true and possible for you?

If you long to hear Jesus' "Well done, good and faithful servant!" and see only gladness on His face, it may be the most important step you ever take.

My Rewards Journal: *What are the "assets" I have in terms of time, talent, and opportunity? How can I invest them for greater results for God's kingdom?*

His divine power has given to us
all things that pertain to life and godliness.

2 Peter 1:3

As each one has received a gift,
minister it to one another,
as good stewards of the manifold grace of God.

1 Peter 4:10

THE JOY SURPRISE

"Blessed are you when they revile and persecute you, and say all kinds of evil against you falsely for My sake. Rejoice and be exceedingly glad, for great is your reward in heaven, for so they persecuted the prophets who were before you."

MATTHEW 5:11–12

Not long ago, I was riding in a van down a hot, dusty road in central India on the way to a small village. I asked our driver how the church where I would be speaking was doing.

"Not good," he said.

"Why not?" I asked.

"Because some who hate our faith are throwing rocks through the windows of the church during services," he said. "They beat up our men in the village. Some believers are now saying it's not worth it to follow Jesus."

A few minutes later, he asked me what I planned to preach on. I told him I had just changed plans! I said, "I want to talk about the secret that made Jesus' followers walk into the arena singing hymns when they knew that lions were waiting to devour them."

Those early martyrs did sing on the way to their deaths, you know. They knew—they were *convinced*—that earth was passing, heaven was lasting. And they believed Jesus when He said that the payment for suffering and rejection for Him in this life would be overwhelming joy in the next.

That's why Peter could encourage persecuted believers:

> Beloved, do not think it strange concerning the fiery trial.... Rejoice to the extent that you partake of Christ's sufferings, that when His glory is revealed, you may also be glad with exceeding joy.
>
> 1 PETER 4:12–13

I'll never forget my visit with that earnest but discouraged group of believers in India. Not one of them felt blessed or joyful. Yet as we spent time together studying what Jesus taught about the connection between sacrifice for Him now and incredible gain later, their outlook changed. They chose to believe Jesus. And even though their trials didn't change one iota, their hopes for the future began to blossom.

Look at another stirring encouragement, from the writer of Hebrews, for those who suffer. Do you see the "joy surprise"?

> But recall the former days in which...you endured a great struggle with sufferings: partly while you were made a spectacle both by reproaches and tribulations, and partly while you became companions of those who were so treated; for you had compassion on me in my chains, and joyfully accepted the plundering of your goods, knowing that you have a better and an enduring possession for yourselves in

heaven. Therefore do not cast away your confidence, which has great reward.

HEBREWS 10:32–35

These followers of Jesus were suffering both for their own choices and for supporting others who were being persecuted. Yet they reacted to plundering (which suggests profound loss of property) with an extraordinary emotion—joyful acceptance.

Did the writer really mean what he said? Yes! The truth of what lay ahead—"an enduring possession for yourselves in heaven"—changed everything.

Christians around the world today are facing profound loss, even death, for the name of Jesus. Maybe you are one. Most of us, though, pay the cost of discipleship in other ways:

- career inequities and mistreatment because of a moral stand on an unpopular issue
- disdain from peers for godly choices in entertainment
- family or social rejection for being an outspoken follower of Jesus

Whatever our situation, if we see only the cost, we will lose the joy. But when we remember our future—and the loving God who guarantees it—the joy is ours to keep.

God is sovereignly at work today to bring each of us important opportunities to impact eternity for Him. Your next opportunity may be cloaked in suffering. If so, I encourage you, my friend, to receive as His word to you today that you "do not cast away your confidence, which has great reward" (Hebrews 10:35).

My Rewards Journal: *Paul wrote, "All who desire to live godly in Christ Jesus will suffer persecution" (2 Timothy 3:12). How might the measure of persecution in my life be an indicator of my commitment to Christ?*

He is no fool who gives what he cannot
keep to gain what he cannot lose.

JIM ELLIOT

For to this end we both labor and suffer reproach,
because we trust in the living God,
who is the Savior of all men, especially of those who believe.

I TIMOTHY 4:10

THE MARK *of a* SERVANT

Whoever desires to become great among you, let him be your servant. And whoever desires to be first among you, let him be your slave—just as the Son of Man did not come to be served, but to serve, and to give His life a ransom for many.

MATTHEW 20:26–28

In her book *The Art of Homemaking,* Edith Schaefer tells the story of how she and her husband, Francis, provided meals for homeless travelers during the Great Depression. They lived near railroad tracks and often heard the knocking at their back door of another hungry hobo looking for a meal.

But Edith did more than push a bean sandwich through the crack in the door. She described a typical tray of food:

> I would butter the bread, cut a lovely big tomato in even slices and pepper them, place them on the bread, and then add bacon. I would sizzle one slice to fold over the tomato and add two leaves of lettuce. For a second sandwich I'd prepare my own favorite: walnut halves stuck into butter, salted on one slice, and then the second piece of buttered bread placed on top. Now for the steaming hot soup....[4]

Her children would often add flowers. Then Edith would add a Gospel of John to the meal before bringing it to the stranger waiting on the back porch.

You can imagine the surprise and pleasure these hungry, lonely men received from Edith's service. Only later did the Schaefers learn that their home had gained a reputation as a home near the rail lines that showed compassion on travelers.

Jesus said, "The Son of Man did not come to be served, but to serve." He fed the hungry. He cared for children. He washed men's dirty feet.

John records that after Jesus had finished washing His disciples' feet, He said, "If I then, your Lord and Teacher, have washed your feet, you also ought to wash one another's feet. For I have given you an example, that you should do as I have done to you" (John 13:14–15).

Serving others for God's glory is how we follow the example and calling of our Lord. And in the kingdom of heaven, serving has great power, and great reward. Jesus said, "If anyone serves Me…him My Father will honor" (John 12:26).

And in the Parable of the Minas, Jesus reveals the exact nature of the surprising reward for faithful service. It is authority, or rulership. The nobleman tells his most faithful and productive servant, "Well done, good servant; because you were faithful in a very little, have authority over ten cities" (Luke 19:17). What a surprising reversal— from servant to ruler!

When I first delved into eternal rewards, I remember thinking, *But I don't want the reward of ruling!* Maybe it doesn't appeal to you either. But rulership as it happens in heaven is a reward we will all want. In fact, I believe that when we are restored to our creation purpose in heaven, we will realize that we have been created by God to exercise leadership for Him.

Genesis tells us that God created humans in His own image and for a particular task—to serve Him by having dominion, or rulership, over the earth. Of course, then came sin. Ever since, the redemptive gift of ruling has often been used for destructive purposes or selfish gain. No wonder we're suspicious of power and those who want it.

But in heaven the curse of sin will be removed. We'll be free to exercise dominion for God to our fullest power while bringing only good to ourselves and others. Serving well here will mean ruling perfectly there.

In today's text, Jesus says, "Whoever desires to become great among you, let him be your servant." Somewhere close at hand today, you and I will find countless opportunities to serve—to lay down our pride, our time, our energy, our resources, and our convenience for someone else.

Jesus showed us what He would do. His invitation to you and me is to stoop to greatness every chance we get.

My Rewards Journal: *How do I feel performing humble or even thankless tasks for others? Who might God ask me to serve more readily on earth as a way to serve Him?*

⌒∞⌒

"*Blessed are those servants whom the master,
when he comes, will find watching.
Assuredly, I say to you that he will gird himself
and have them sit down to eat, and will come and serve them.*"

Luke 12:37

DOUBLE PAYCHECK

Bondservants, obey in all things your masters according to the flesh, not with eyeservice, as men-pleasers, but in sincerity of heart, fearing God. And whatever you do, do it heartily, as to the Lord and not to men, knowing that from the Lord you will receive the reward of the inheritance; for you serve the Lord Christ. But he who does wrong will be repaid for what he has done, and there is no partiality.

Colossians 3:22–25

God will reward you if you die for Him as a martyr. But will He reward you, or even notice, if you serve Him faithfully in a demeaning job? Today's verse makes an incredible claim—that you can work wholeheartedly at the most demeaning task for the least appreciative boss, knowing that "you will receive the reward."

Some time ago, I led a seminar for a group of well-educated, optimistic young businessmen and businesswomen in the Far East. Their positive attitudes contrasted sharply with their negative circumstances. They told me that they suffered from discrimination because of their faith, including officially sanctioned mistreatment by their bosses on a daily basis.

During a break, I pulled aside one of the conferees and asked, "How does your group maintain such a great attitude about their work?"

"Well," he answered, "many of us have an important secret. We don't really work for our boss. We work instead 'heartily, as to the Lord.' God is a much better employer!"

Those believers were operating on the biblical principle of honoring your employer by serving him in Christ's name. And this is just religious jargon. Notice in today's verses from Colossians that Paul carefully describes what serving "as to the Lord" would look like: "obey in all things," "not...as men-pleasers," "in sincerity of heart," and "fearing God."

In other words, don't just pretend to please those you serve. Make it real.

The first secret of enjoying your job, as those believers were proving, is to know whom you actually work for. You are working for Jesus, and knowing that, you can really put your heart into it.

But there is a second secret. And that afternoon in the Far East, we uncovered it together. Paul goes on to say, "Knowing that from the Lord *you will receive the reward* of the inheritance; for you serve the Lord Christ" (v. 24).

We know that the "reward of the inheritance" Paul describes cannot refer to salvation, because salvation is never described as a reward for our work but as a gift from God by His grace. The second secret, then, is that you will receive a "second paycheck" from God later: You get paid once for a task by your earthly boss (who may not treat or pay you fairly), but you can get paid a second time for the same task by your heavenly boss (who will always treat you fairly and reward you generously in heaven).

This principle of double payment applies to us in the many roles where we are called on to honor God by rendering submissive service—as homemakers, church workers, neighbors, family members, and friends. Our real "boss" is God. And He is such a gracious and generous boss that He has chosen to credit our account in Heaven for how we serve on earth, if only we will do it "unto Him."

The reward for faithful, submissive service is up to you today. And it's a reward that the "Boss of heaven" longs to give. Jesus knows that faith would be required to even believe that His rewards exist. Maybe that's why His final words—as recorded on the last page of the Bible—show how eager He is to show His appreciation:

"And behold, I am coming quickly, and My reward is with Me, to give to every one according to his work."

REVELATION 22:12

God cares. God notices your humble service today in His name. And God can't wait to reward you.

My Rewards Journal: *Who are the people God has asked me to "work" for? How might imagining Jesus in their place change my attitudes or habits or approach?*

✑

Then I heard a voice from heaven say,
"Write: Blessed are the dead who die in the Lord from now on."
"Yes," says the Spirit, "they will rest from their labor,
or their deeds will follow them."

Revelation 14:13, NIV

And whatever you do in word or deed,
do all in the name of the Lord Jesus,
giving thanks to God the Father through Him.

Colossians 3:17

GOD'S SECRET SERVICE

"Take heed that you do not do your charitable deeds before men, to be seen by them. Otherwise you have no reward from your Father in heaven. Therefore, when you do a charitable deed, do not sound a trumpet before you as the hypocrites do in the synagogues and in the streets, that they may have glory from men. Assuredly, I say to you, they have their reward. But when you do a charitable deed, do not let your left hand know what your right hand is doing, that your charitable deed may be in secret; and your Father who sees in secret will Himself reward you openly."

MATTHEW 6:1–4

One of the reasons some Christians shy away from giving good works a good name is that those who emphasize works often give them a bad one. Good works too easily become a substitute gospel, or the measure of personal acceptability to God, or the mark of status in the community.

But the priority of good works in a believer's life is a major theme in the New Testament. They don't earn us our new life in Christ, but they are the natural and highly desirable expression of it. Here are four examples:

- And God is able to make all grace abound toward you, that you…may have an abundance for every good work. (2 Corinthians 9:8)
- That you may walk worthy of the Lord, fully pleasing Him, being fruitful in every good work. (Colossians 1:10)
- May our Lord Jesus Christ himself…encourage your hearts and strengthen you in every good deed and word. (2 Thessalonians 2:16–17, NIV)
- Remind them…to be ready for every good work. (Titus 3:1)

Are you suspicious of "do-gooders" and therefore find yourself responding cautiously to what Jesus said about good works and eternal reward?

Consider joining God's secret service today.

Jesus identified secrecy as a practical but powerful test for whether a work was God-honoring. Interestingly, those professional do-gooders of His day, the Pharisees, would have none of it!

They specialized in getting the most public credit possible for every personal religious act. Today's text describes their practice of sounding a trumpet to let others know when they were giving. Many considered them to be the epitome of spirituality. But Jesus said, "Do not do your charitable deeds before men, to be seen by them. Otherwise you have no reward from your Father in heaven."

Today you will have many opportunities to serve others in the name of Jesus. Practice invisibility! Render a good work by stealth. Even better, do your good work in such a way that you are unnoticed *and* God gets the glory.

I know a men's group that decided to ask a bold question: *What could we do within five blocks of our church that would greatly enhance God's reputation without bringing credit to any individual?* They decided that, for them, this would mean not even directing attention to their church.

Then they made a plan and implemented it. They gave and witnessed anonymously. They intervened and advocated behind the scenes without pay. They made repairs secretly. They left food on doorsteps...all as secret agents for Jesus Christ.

"We tried to do things in such a way that a person couldn't help exclaiming in thanks to God," one said later. "We learned a few things about what it means to be an angel—a messenger or servant for God who has an unseen but dramatic impact on a person in need. What an adventure it was!"

Pastor Mark Buchanan writes in *Your God Is Too Safe,* "Either we do good things in order to be seen by others, or we do them in order to bring praise to God. Secrecy is one of the most profound theological statements we can make. It is acting on the belief that the *reward of God* matters more than the *reward of man.* It is trusting in the trustworthiness of God" (emphasis added).[5]

Is God calling you to be zealous about good works for Him today? Don't be shy. Be invisible.

My Rewards Journal: *Jesus said that even fasting and praying are rewardable when done in private (Matthew 6:6, 18). How does this change the way I think about my spiritual disciplines?*

Seek secrecy for your good deeds. Do not even see your own virtue.
Hide from yourself that which you yourself have done that is
commendable; for the proud contemplation of your own generosity may
tarnish all your alms. Keep the thing so secret that even you yourself are
hardly aware that you are doing anything at all praiseworthy.
Let God be present, and you will have enough of an audience.
He will reward you, reward you "openly," reward you as a Father
rewards a child, reward you as one who saw what you did,
and knew that you did it wholly unto him.

CHARLES SPURGEON

He who looks into the perfect law of liberty
and continues in it, and is not a forgetful hearer
but a doer of the work, this one will be blessed in what he does.

JAMES 1:25

THE MAN GOD CALLED "FOOL"

Then He spoke a parable to them, saying: "The ground of a certain rich man yielded plentifully. And he thought within himself, saying, 'What shall I do, since I have no room to store my crops?' So he said, 'I will do this: I will pull down my barns and build greater, and there I will store all my crops and my goods. And I will say to my soul, "Soul, you have many goods laid up for many years; take your ease; eat, drink, and be merry."'"
LUKE 12:16–19

At the time of Christ, people thought about money the same way most people do today: *You can't take it with you, so you should get all you can here and enjoy it while you can.* In fact, in New Testament times a man's prosperity was often considered an indication of his spiritual condition and a measure of his favor with God.

In this context, Jesus' teachings about money and possessions must have been shocking indeed. To a rich young man who seemed to be living a perfect life, Jesus said, "Sell all that you have and distribute to the poor" (Luke 18:22).

Unfortunately, some today have concluded that it's unspiritual for Christians to care about treasure. But while Jesus warned that idolizing money will turn a person away from God, He never taught that owning it is wrong. Instead, He stressed that we should manage our money in such a way that we can take it with us when we go!

He said:

> "Do not lay up for yourselves treasures on earth, where moth and rust destroy and where thieves break in and steal; but *lay up for yourselves treasures in heaven.*"

MATTHEW 6:19–21

Is laying up treasure in heaven just an option for the super spiritual among us? No. As we saw in *A Life God Rewards,* the construction "lay up" in the Greek is to be taken as a command from God. To drive this point home, Jesus told a story about a wealthy person who did *not* lay up treasure in heaven.

He is the man God called a fool.

As we see in today's text, everything he touched seemed to come up money. Even his investment strategy seems sensible: build a bigger nest egg, take more time off, and enjoy yourself more.

But Jesus said:

> "God said to him, 'Fool! This night your soul will be required of you; then whose will those things be which you have provided?' So is he who lays up treasure for himself, and is not rich toward God."

LUKE 12:20–21

The fool's mistake was to single-mindedly store up wealth on earth without storing up any in heaven. Jesus wasn't teaching that we shouldn't wisely tend our personal assets. But if storing it up here is all we do, we're foolish *because we will lose it all in the end.*

Jesus gave some practical advice on how to manage our material resources: *First, to have all you need here, serve God first* (Matthew 6:33; Luke 12:31). *Then, to take your treasure to heaven, give some of it away to God's work here.* He said, "Sell what you have and give alms; provide yourselves money bags which do not grow old, a treasure in the heavens that does not fail, where no thief approaches nor moth destroys" (Luke 12:33).

Notice the clear connection between *giving away your money to the needy here* and *providing treasure that lasts for yourselves in heaven.* We see the connection again in Paul's advice to Timothy. Command those who are wealthy, he said, to "do good, that they be rich in good works, ready to give, willing to share, storing up for themselves a good foundation for the time to come"(1 Timothy 6:18–19).

The fool in Jesus' story slipped into an earthbound lie we all recognize. He thought that treasure here was the *real* treasure. Think about how you manage your money and possessions today. Are you investing for maximum return here or in eternity?

Your real and lasting treasure is in heaven, and Jesus wants you to have a lot of it when you get there.

MY REWARDS JOURNAL: *If I had to guess, how much treasure would I say I have stored up in heaven right now? How will knowing about treasure in heaven change my habits?*

❧

We ask how much a man gives;
Christ asks how much he keeps.

ANDREW MURRAY

A RADICAL LIFE

Then Jesus said to His disciples, "If anyone desires to come after Me, let him deny himself, and take up his cross, and follow Me. For whoever desires to save his life will lose it, but whoever loses his life for My sake will find it. For what profit is it to a man if he gains the whole world, and loses his own soul? Or what will a man give in exchange for his soul? For the Son of Man will come in the glory of His Father with His angels, and then He will reward each according to his works."

MATTHEW 16:24–27

When Jesus defined what it means to live a life on earth for Him that will add up to reward in eternity, He began with this radical statement:

> "If anyone desires to come after Me, let him deny himself, and take up his cross, and follow Me."
>
> MATTHEW 16:24

Deny yourself. Take up your cross. Lose your life. What did Jesus mean? Certainly nothing like "Join my organization" or "Start coming to my church." Here, Jesus was defining discipleship in the most radical terms—a life for a life.

But they are terms we can easily gloss over or miss altogether. The phrase "my cross to bear," which has come to us from this verse, gets watered down to mean an annoying inconvenience or disadvantage (for example, you're sure your nose is too large, or your obnoxious neighbor has no plans of ever moving).

But Jesus meant something else entirely, and His disciples would have understood it immediately: chained men condemned to die, dragging their own crosses to the place of execution. Roman crosses were heavy and rough. Carrying them was shaming, exhausting, and ultimately crushing.

One day the disciples would see that Jesus had been describing His own death.

But friend, just as radical as Jesus' invitation to give up our life for Him is His promise of why such an act could actually add up to "profit": *because it is the only way to save your life, and because of what He will do for you in eternity.*

Jesus revealed what He would do:

"The Son of Man will come in the glory of His Father with His angels, and then He will reward each according to his works."

v. 27

You see, Jesus is proposing a very personal exchange—your life now for His reward later. And He wants every follower to know that if you agree to such a radical exchange, you *will* find the life you're really looking for, now and in eternity.

We can talk about the Christian life from many perspectives— good friends, good fellowship, emotionally satisfying worship, personal healing, wise living. But those are by-products. First, we are called to a radical and very personal exchange.

Let me ask you today: Have you opened your heart and mind to hear Jesus' call—every radical, personal possibility of it?

Here are some discipleship choices I have seen put into action recently. I list them as a challenge and an invitation for you to think and pray about:

- Decide to live on 10 percent of your income, and give 90 percent to God. Adjust your standard of living to make it possible. Expect joy.
- Give over your house, or a room of it, completely to God's work. Accept people in your home you might not otherwise welcome. Ask, *What does Jesus want to do with this room this week?*
- Pray six hours every day.
- Submit to a difficult and unfair person in authority because behind that person you see Christ, your true Master.
- Ask, "How can I use my work skills to benefit God's work in a more direct way?"
- Give your most prized possession to a person who would prize it more.
- Turn your next family vacation into a missions trip.
- Research and write up a realistic skills-for-ministry training plan that you can accomplish within twelve months. Implement a similar plan every year from now on.
- Trade your TV-watching time for eternal reward. Use the time to invest in people's lives. Start with your family; then move outward to others. Keep a log of what God is doing.

- Negotiate a four-day/ten-hour-a-day workweek so you can devote one full day a week to ministry.
- Call your pastor and tell him you're available for the next important task that no one else will volunteer for. Take it, no exceptions.
- Fast one day a week. Pray and read your Bible on your knees when you would normally be eating.

These followers of Jesus are making choices that will echo through eternity, and you can too. Each choice begins by understanding what it means to follow Jesus, and then doing so, with your eyes on Him and your hopes in eternity.

My Rewards Journal: *What "radical" kind of living for Christ have I done in the past? How did that feel? What is keeping me from making radical choices for Him today?*

Do all the good you can, by all the means you can,
in all the ways you can, in all the places you can,
at all the times you can to all the people
you can as long as ever you can!

John Wesley

Week Four

∞

AT HOME IN
HEAVEN

"I go to prepare a place for you....
That where I am, there you may be also."

JOHN 14:2–3

HEAVEN IS *a* REAL PLACE

Then he said to Jesus, "Lord, remember me when You come into Your
kingdom." And Jesus said to him, "Assuredly, I say to you, today you will
be with Me in Paradise."

LUKE 23:42–43

When I was a boy, the thought of heaven used to frighten me
more than the thought of hell," confessed David Lloyd
George, a British prime minister from the nineteenth century. "I pictured heaven as a place where time would be perpetual Sundays, with
perpetual services from which there would be no escape. It was a hor-
rible nightmare...and made me an atheist for ten years."

Can you relate? I can. I grew up hearing about a heaven full of
angel choirs waving palm branches. It sounded like one long choir
practice.

In this fourth week of readings, we'll look at what Jesus revealed
about eternity, asking questions like: What will heaven (and hell) be
like? How will rewards change our experience there? Will heaven be
different for different people?

Take a minute to identify what comes to mind when you hear
the word *heaven*. I often hear responses like:

- Clouds
- Rest (young moms feel strongly about this one)
- Pearly gates
- Time to visit with family and friends you haven't seen for a while (a favorite with grandparents)
- Moses (looking a lot like Charlton Heston)
- Being with Jesus
- The perfect dream

Heaven matters, and what we believe about it has the power to change what we do one minute from now. But what is the truth about heaven?

Jesus spoke often and matter-of-factly about it. He described it as the home of God the Father and His angels, the place where Jesus would sit on a throne to judge and rule, and the highly desired destination for all His followers.

So much about our lives in heaven remains unknown—we *can't* know it because we are limited by our earthly understandings. But today I want you to consider that heaven is not a dream, a movie fantasy, or a spiritual idea. It is a real place.

Yet somehow when we think of heaven, we imagine "sweet nothingness." No wonder some people think heaven will be boring!

Consider the paradise God created for man in the Garden of Eden. Adam and Eve didn't sing in a choir all day. They had purpose, work, opportunity, fellowship, responsibility, pleasure, and fulfillment. Why should it be otherwise in heaven? Our God is purposeful, at work, relational, creative....

Some of the descriptions of heaven in the New Testament are

striking for their concreteness and familiarity. For example:

- *Residences.* "In My Father's house are many mansions; if it were not so, I would have told you. I go to prepare a place for you" (John 14:2).

- *Streets and gates.* "The twelve gates were twelve pearls: each individual gate was of one pearl. And the street of the city was pure gold" (Revelation 21:21).

- *River, trees, and fruit.* "In the middle of its street, and on either side of the river, was the tree of life, which bore twelve fruits, each tree yielding its fruit every month" (Revelation 22:2).

- *Fellowship with other believers.* "You have come…to the city of the living God, the heavenly Jerusalem, to an innumerable company of angels, to the general assembly and church of the firstborn who are registered in heaven" (Hebrews 12:22–23).

- *Serving.* "And there shall be no more curse, but the throne of God and of the Lamb shall be in it, and His servants shall serve Him" (Revelation 22:3).

- *Eating.* "Blessed are those who are called to the marriage supper of the Lamb!" (Revelation 19:9).

- *Fellowship and closeness with God.* "Today you will be with Me in Paradise" (Luke 23:43).

- *Praise and worship.* "Then a voice came from the throne, saying, 'Praise our God, all you His servants and those who fear Him, both small and great!'" (Revelation 19:5).

- *Rest and reward.* "Write: 'Blessed are the dead who die in the Lord from now on.' 'Yes,' says the Spirit, 'that they may rest from their labors, and their works follow them'" (Revelation 14:13).

As you go about your ordinary day, remember that one day you too will be able to experience the fulfillment of Jesus' personal invitation to be with Him in heaven. What a new—and very real—beginning it will be! And it has not entered into *any* human mind what God has prepared for you there (1 Corinthians 2:9).

Jesus did not reach out to comfort the dying thief on the cross next to Him with the promise of a dream. Jesus promised him something real: "Assuredly, I say to you, today you will be with Me in Paradise" (Luke 23:43). And you can live in the certainty today that Jesus did not die so you could live forever in one either.

MY REWARDS JOURNAL: *How is what the Bible says about heaven different from what I grew up believing? How do I feel about heaven as the Bible describes it?*

⌀

Be faithful until death,
and I will give you the crown of life.

REVELATION 2:10

Now hope does not disappoint,
because the love of God has been poured out in our hearts
by the Holy Spirit who was given to us.

ROMANS 5:5

FAMILY REUNION

Beloved, now we are children of God; and it has not yet been revealed what we shall be, but we know that when He is revealed, we shall be like Him, for we shall see Him as He is. And everyone who has this hope in Him purifies himself, just as He is pure.

1 JOHN 3:2–3

Heaven is the chosen site for God's family reunion, and the whole human race is invited. For those of us who accept His invitation, our present, daily existence is but a temporary mission of preparation until we journey home. Some of our travel is exhilarating, some full of difficulties.

But one day our journey will end. We will pass over from death to life. We will be at home with God… Astonishing!

Consider today some of the wonders Scripture records about our homecoming:

1. *We will all feel God's welcome.* Jesus said, "I go to prepare a place for you…that where I am, there you may be also" (John 14:2–3). Heaven will feel like home to every child of God. Like a tender father waiting at the front door in the evening, He will *first*

express delight at our arrival (even if we arrive with mud on our shoes or skinned knees). We will equally sense God's anticipation and pleasure in our company.

2. *We will all be changed.* In today's text we read, "It has not yet been revealed what we shall be, but we know that when He is revealed, we shall be like Him, for we shall see Him as He is" (v. 2). Paul looked forward to the time when "we shall be changed. For this corruptible must put on incorruption, and this mortal must put on immortality" (1 Corinthians 15:52–53).

3. *We will all worship.* Worship will be the natural, unstoppable response we have to the direct experience of God and His goodness. In heaven, as we enjoy the fullness of God, we will naturally breathe out thankfulness, adoration, and praise (Revelation 19:6–7).

4. *We will all experience the end of suffering.* In heaven, there will be no more pain, sorrow, hunger, thirst, loneliness, want, sin, death—no more suffering of any kind (Revelation 21:4).

Together we'll have an eternity to be astounded at "the things which God has prepared for those who love Him" (1 Corinthians 2:9).

But what might God be asking you and me to do today in light of our remarkable future? The apostles linked two key responses directly to the truth about heaven:

- *Our hope of heaven beckons us to purify ourselves.* To live as children of God with the promise of an amazing future can change you today. John wrote, "We shall see Him as He is. And everyone who has this hope in Him purifies himself, just as He is pure" (1 John 3:2–3).

Try reminding yourself today that you *will* see Jesus face-to-face. That you *will* live in His presence as a heavenly being. Just the knowledge of that lasting reality can make the lure of passing sins less enticing, more obviously deceitful and costly.

- *Our hope of reward beckons us to serve God.* After Paul had told the Corinthians how central their faith was to the reality of the resurrection, he concluded, "Therefore, my beloved brethren, be steadfast, immovable, always abounding in the work of the Lord, knowing that your labor is not in vain in the Lord" (1 Corinthians 15:58).

Today is another gift from God. You and I can easily let it slip past, forgetting about its opportunity, missing the prize of eternity wrapped in the gift of hours.

Or we can faithfully and joyfully serve God in every way possible, knowing that every deed in His name will count eternally on that wonderful day when we all meet at God's family reunion.

MY REWARDS JOURNAL: *"Dear Lord, how thankful I am to be part of Your family. Help me to behave like a child of Yours today."*

❧

As for me, I will see Your face in righteousness;
I shall be satisfied when I awake in Your likeness.

PSALM 17:15

While women weep as they do now,
I'll fight; while little children go hungry, as they do now,
I'll fight; while men go to prison, in and out, in and out,
as they do now, I'll fight; while there is a drunkard left,
while there is a poor lost girl upon the streets,
while there remains one dark soul without the light of God,
I'll fight—I'll fight to the very end.

WILLIAM BOOTH, FOUNDER OF THE SALVATION ARMY

WONDERFUL *for* ALL (*and* EVEN BETTER *for* SOME)

"And I bestow upon you a kingdom, just as My Father bestowed one upon Me, that you may eat and drink at My table in My kingdom, and sit on thrones judging the twelve tribes of Israel."

LUKE 22:29–30

In *The Prayer of Jabez*, we saw that God wants us to ask Him— again and again—for abundant blessing in this life. In *A Life God Rewards* and in this devotional, I hope you've seen that God wants you to work hard for Him now, knowing that He will reward you abundantly in the life to come.

Today I want to focus on the flip side of God's plan: *If blessing and reward come to those who earnestly ask and work, some blessings and some rewards will not come to those who do not seek them.*

Jesus never flinched when His disciples asked Him, "See, we have left all and followed You. *Therefore what shall we have?*" (Matthew 19:27). Instead of lecturing the disciples about expecting too much from Him, Jesus responded with a guarantee. "Assuredly I say to you," He began. Then He told them that after the resurrection, they would sit on twelve thrones and judge Israel. And He promised even more: To "everyone" who had left all to follow Him, a payback was in store that would be a hundredfold more than anything they could otherwise receive (vv. 28–29).

But clearly then while some will rule and reign in heaven, others will not. Some will receive rewards that will make them "exceedingly glad" (Matthew 5:12), and some will not.

And, therefore, heaven will not be experienced the same by everyone.

Does this statement surprise you? When I teach this message, I hear reactions like, "I don't want a heaven where there is a hierarchy—we have enough of that on earth." Or, "A heaven that isn't the same for everyone just wouldn't feel like heaven to me."

Perhaps you grew up thinking that heaven operated like a large communal farm—equal pay, common tasks, and evenly distributed returns. But this thinking has no basis in Scripture. And as fair and pleasant as it sounds, communism wouldn't work in heaven any better than it has on earth.

After the former Soviet Union dissolved, I visited with workers in one of the republics. Their productivity and quality standards had fallen far behind the rest of the industrialized world. When I asked one worker why the system had failed, he told me, "It makes no difference if I work hard all day, or sit down and don't work all day. Nothing changes. They pretend to pay us, and we pretend to work."

Would any of us rise to our best under those circumstances? God made humans to be highly motivated when we can see positive results for our actions. We operate by the same laws of consequences in our families, classrooms, companies, and nations.

If heaven were the same for everyone, it would mean that nothing I do on earth will ultimately matter and that I am not personally responsible to my Creator. Instead, God makes it clear that even though heaven will be wonderful for all, it will be still better for some.

If you plan to live a life that God rewards, this comes as *good* news!

While sin pollutes our responses to accomplishments, leadership, and wealth on earth, none of that will exist in heaven. Each of us will be overwhelmed by the glory of the Lord, the greatness of His generosity, and the inarguable "rightness" of His justice.

In fact, we should never presume to tell God that He can't make things fair for every person, no matter what their special circumstances might be. Our God has staked His very reputation on His unfailing righteousness, justice, mercy, and truth (Jeremiah 9:24; Psalm 89:14).

This is the awesome God who will personally, graciously, and joyfully reward His children "each according to his works" (Matthew 16:27). And His "Well done, good and faithful servant" will echo like the sweetest music to our ears for all eternity.

MY REWARDS JOURNAL: *What do I believe will be the best thing about being in heaven?*

❦

*There are many mansions in God's house because heaven
is intended for various degrees of honor and blessedness.
Some are designed to sit in higher places there than others;
some are designed to be advanced to higher degrees of
honor and glory than others are; and, therefore,
there are various mansions, and some more honorable
mansions and seats, in heaven than others.
Though they are all seats of exceeding honor
and blessedness yet some more so than others.*

JONATHAN EDWARDS

HOMESICK *for* HEAVEN

For we who are in this tent groan, being burdened, not because we want to be unclothed, but further clothed, that mortality may be swallowed up by life.

2 CORINTHIANS 5:4

Do you believe you were made for heaven—or for earth?

Right now, you live in a remarkable physical body, with all its needs and hungers directing your attention toward everything you can see, taste, and touch. Life on earth is so real, isn't it? And heaven so…out there! It's hard to imagine you could belong *there* when *here* is so convincing.

But I want to show you today that although God equipped you to live on earth, He really made you for heaven. And it is heaven you long for most, whether or not you know it yet.

If you're familiar with C. S. Lewis's allegorical series The Chronicles of Narnia, you know about the great lion Aslan. In *The Last Battle,* the final book in the series, Aslan introduces us to the New Narnia, a picture of heaven:

The new Narnia…was a deeper country: every rock and flower and blade of grass looked as if it meant more. I can't describe it any better than that: if you ever get there, you will know what I mean.

It was the Unicorn who summed up what everyone was feeling. He stamped his right forehoof on the ground and neighed and then cried:

"I have come home at last! This is my real country! I belong here. This is the land I have been looking for all my life, though I never knew it till now. The reason why we loved the old Narnia is that it sometimes looked a little like this."[6]

Lewis imagined that when we see heaven, it would be wonderful beyond description and yet strangely familiar. So familiar that we will recognize it as our true home. So wonderful that it will answer every need and desire we ever had on earth.

The apostle Paul said many of the same things about heaven, and he wasn't just using his imagination. Paul reports in 2 Corinthians 12 that he knew "a man in Christ" who was "caught up into Paradise" (vv. 2, 4). Most scholars are convinced that Paul himself was the man.

So what *did* Paul see? He couldn't put it in words because of what one commentator calls our "unacquaintedness with the language of the upper world." Yet Paul's powerful longing for heaven says a great deal:

- "For in this we groan, earnestly desiring to be clothed with our habitation which is from heaven" (2 Corinthians 5:2).
- "For we who are in this tent groan, being burdened, not because we want to be unclothed, but further clothed, that mortality may be swallowed up by life" (2 Corinthians 5:4).

- "We also who have the firstfruits of the Spirit, even we our-selves groan within ourselves, eagerly waiting for the adoption, the redemption of our body" (Romans 8:23).

Notice the words *groan, earnestly desiring,* and *eagerly waiting.* Paul sounds like he was homesick for heaven, doesn't he? And could it be that you are too?

Today, as you look at your life, how would you describe your deepest desire? Could it be that you ache for an experience and a place that earth can't provide?

You see, that deep hunger can be one of God's greatest invita-tions to you. If you allow that yearning to turn your heart fully toward heaven—eagerly reaching for what is invisible, *but more real* than what you see—you will have discovered one of the biggest keys to living a life God rewards.

Paul's longing for heaven served as a constant reminder to him that he was made for there, not here. This knowledge shaped his pri-orities. It focused his aims. It caused him to view his sufferings and trials as light and momentary when compared to what heaven promised (2 Corinthians 4:17–18).

In *A Life God Rewards,* I encouraged you to change your citizen-ship to heaven. Today, I invite you to let your longing for that deeper country motivate you to live for it with great passion. Let your hunger keep you reaching with all your heart for all He has for you right now and one day in heaven.

MY REWARDS JOURNAL: *"Dear Lord, help me to recognize my hunger for heaven for what it really is! Show me when I'm reaching for a counterfeit cure, rather than for my real future."*

⸻

Not that I wish the groaning to cease. My hope, indeed, is that it deepens. My hope is that we learn to join our groaning, pitch for pitch and rhythm for rhythm, to the groaning of all creation—earth and sky, waterfall and water buffalo, chickadee and katydid, stone and tree—to all things as they wait for the sons of God to be revealed (see Romans 8:22).
Groaning is creation's song, the blues of the cosmos, and we're to hum its melody and take up its chorus.

MARK BUCHANAN

For those who say such things declare plainly that they seek a homeland. And truly if they had called to mind that country from which they had come out, they would have had opportunity to return. But now they desire a better, that is, a heavenly country. Therefore God is not ashamed to be called their God, for He has prepared a city for them.

HEBREWS 11:14–16

Hell Is No Party

"There was a certain rich man who was clothed in purple and fine linen and fared sumptuously every day. But there was a certain beggar named Lazarus, full of sores, who was laid at his gate, desiring to be fed with the crumbs which fell from the rich man's table. Moreover the dogs came and licked his sores. So it was that the beggar died, and was carried by the angels to Abraham's bosom. The rich man also died and was buried. And being in torments in Hades, he lifted up his eyes and saw Abraham afar off, and Lazarus in his bosom."

Luke 16:19–23

Before Timothy McVeigh was executed for killing 168 innocent people with a bomb, he said, "If I'm going to hell, I'm gonna have a lot of company."

Will hell be the place where the company makes up for the misery, one big party, as some seem to think?

Jesus wanted all His followers to know the truth about hell. One day He told a story that followed two people to their eternal destinations. The first was a rich man who enjoyed the best of everything. The other was a miserable beggar named Lazarus who lived off the crumbs that fell from the rich man's table.

But when the two men died, things changed. The beggar went to eternal comfort in heaven—in Jesus' story called "Abraham's bosom." The rich man went to eternal misery in hell.

That's when the real drama begins. As today's passage shows, the rich man in hell could see all the way to heaven. There, he saw that Lazarus was being comforted. And now it was his turn to beg. I'll paraphrase the conversation that follows (vv. 24–31):

Rich man: "Father Abraham, have mercy on me! Send Lazarus with a drop of water to cool my tongue, for I am tormented in this flame!"

Abraham: "Lazarus can't come to you because between you and us there is an impassable gulf."

Rich man: "Then I beg you to send Lazarus to earth to talk to my five brothers. Otherwise, they'll end up in this place of torment, too!"

Abraham: "They already have the Scriptures to show them the truth about hell if they want to hear it."

Rich man: "Yes, but if someone goes from the dead to talk to my brothers, I *know* they'll repent!"

Abraham: "If they won't believe what the Bible says, neither will they believe a witness from the dead...."

What a sobering view into eternity! And what a promising revelation for today, if we receive and act on what Jesus came to tell us!

In His story, I find clear and critical information about hell and the link between our today and our forever:

1. *Death is the door between our life now and our life later.* When we pass through it, we leave behind any opportunity to change our eternity. After that, "there is a great gulf fixed" (v. 26).

2.   *Hell is a place of torment without an exit.* People there are conscious, they can communicate, they feel pain and regret—and their condition will never change. Once you enter, you can never leave.

3.   *In our life later, God will bring final justice to every human being.* Interestingly, the rich man—once he can look back on his life—never argues with God over where his choices have taken him. This makes sense: The essence of judgment, after all, isn't harshness but applying justice in such a way that things are made right. In fact, Jesus on other occasions revealed that just as there will be degrees of reward in heaven, so there will be degrees of suffering in hell (see Matthew 11:23–24; 23:14; Romans 2:5). God cares about the inequities and suffering in our lives and in our world. One day, His judgments will make things right.

4.   *Our life now has a direct effect on our life later.* Its consequences are predictable and final, and they will matter to us forever.

Imagine what the rich man and Lazarus would say to you if you met on a street corner today. Would each man's advice to you be different or the same?

I imagine they might bring the very same, urgent message: *Life is short, but God is good. Accept Jesus as your Lord and Savior. Live for an eternity with Him. Spread the news.*

MY REWARDS JOURNAL: *"Lord, how wonderful it is to know that no matter what things look like now, one day You will make everything right for everyone. This is especially encouraging when I see _____."*

God is a righteous ruler; all His laws are holy, just, and good...
He is impartial and uniform in their execution.
As a judge He renders unto every man according to His works.
He neither condemns the innocent, nor clears the guilty.

CHARLES HODGES

Conversely, when we see the righteous brought into affliction by the
ungodly, assailed with injuries, overwhelmed with calumnies,
and lacerated by insult and contumely, while, on the contrary,
the wicked flourish, prosper, acquire ease and honour,
and all these with impunity, we ought forthwith to infer that there
will be a future life in which iniquity shall receive its punishment,
and righteousness its reward.

JOHN CALVIN

AMBASSADORS

Therefore, if anyone is in Christ, he is a new creation; old things have passed away; behold, all things have become new. Now all things are of God, who has reconciled us to Himself through Jesus Christ, and has given us the ministry of reconciliation, that is, that God was in Christ reconciling the world to Himself, not imputing their trespasses to them, and has committed to us the word of reconciliation. Now then, we are ambassadors for Christ, as though God were pleading through us: we implore you on Christ's behalf, be reconciled to God.

2 Corinthians 5:17–20

I read once that looking at the stars through a telescope on earth is a little like looking up from the bottom of a swimming pool. No matter how hard you squint, objects still look pretty blurry (that's why stars twinkle). The vast ocean of atmosphere above us limits how clearly a telescope can see.

No wonder astronomers were excited when, in 1990, they launched the Hubble Space Telescope. Hubble, which is the size of a school bus, studies the stars from an orbit *above* Earth's atmosphere. No blur. No twinkle. Almost every week, scientists are making new discoveries.

Letting Jesus show us the facts about eternity is a little like that. Our perspective is limited, but His is not. He came from eternity to show us the truth. And if we truly receive what He came to earth to reveal, we'll never look at our life here in the same way again.

Or other people.

Is the truth about eternity changing how you think about your purpose on earth today? Then you *must* see other people differently, too.

When C. S. Lewis wrote his essay "The Weight of Glory," about what he called "the overwhelming possibilities" of eternity, he concluded: "There are no ordinary people. You have never talked to a mere mortal. Nations, cultures, arts, civilizations—these are mortal, and their life is to ours as the life of a gnat. But it is immortals whom we joke with, work with, marry, snub, and exploit—immortal horrors or everlasting splendours."[7]

Friend, that is why telling and living the Good News of the Gospel today to other "immortals" is the most important eternal work we can do. There's no greater gift we could pass on to the people we live with, work with, or meet on the street.

Every person has eternal possibilities.

Paul's encounter with Christ changed his viewpoint radically. It persuaded him that "those who live should live no longer for themselves," and "therefore, from now on, we regard no one according to the flesh" (2 Corinthians 5:15–16).

Paul described this amazing assignment as being an ambassador for Christ. Each day, Paul said, we should realize that Christ has commissioned us to make His appeal *on His behalf* to the world. The

Bible clearly describes that our King is "not willing that any should perish but that all should come to repentance" (2 Peter 3:9).

The next time you walk out of your house or office, consider how a personal assignment as Christ's ambassador would shape your day.

- You are specially commissioned to spread the message of your King.
- You should expect many opportunities to bring reconciliation between your King and those who oppose Him, or ignore Him, or are simply ignorant of Him.
- You should remember that your words and your example speak loudly about your King and the significance of His message.
- You should keep in mind that ambassadors only succeed if they put their King's interests and priorities before their personal affairs.

Ask God today to give you a greater passion for souls. It's a passion that could change eternity for many other immortals, and bring you great reward, too. Jesus told His disciples, "He who reaps receives wages, and gathers fruit for eternal life, that both he who sows and he who reaps may rejoice together" (John 4:36).

You have been called and commissioned for a joyful task. Jesus has shown you the truth, and the truth has set you free to spread the word.

MY REWARDS JOURNAL: *What three names come to mind right now of people I should pray about and plan to share the Gospel with this week?*

∽✺∽

Even if we persuade only a few,
we shall obtain very great rewards, for,
like good laborers, we shall receive recompense from the Master.

JUSTIN MARTYR

Those who are wise shall shine
Like the brightness of the firmament,
And those who turn many to righteousness
Like the stars forever and ever.

DANIEL 12:3

For what is our hope, or joy, or crown of rejoicing?
Is it not even you in the presence of our Lord Jesus Christ at His coming?

1 THESSALONIANS 2:19

THE CONTEST *of* YOUR LIFE

Therefore, since we are surrounded by such a great cloud of witnesses, let us throw off everything that hinders and the sin that so easily entangles, and let us run with perseverance the race marked out for us. Let us fix our eyes on Jesus, the author and perfecter of our faith, who for the joy set before him endured the cross, scorning its shame, and sat down at the right hand of the throne of God.

HEBREWS 12:1–2, NIV

I t had to be one of the best moments in Olympic history. Maybe you saw it on TV. Sarah Hughes, then a high school junior from Great Neck, New York, was in fourth place in the final round of the figure skating competition. To win a metal, she'd need a miracle. She'd have to give the performance of her life—and then some.

As her turn approached, she decided to forget the pressure and just skate for the pure joy of it. During the whole performance, she grinned from ear to ear. And she made history—for one thing, she was the first Olympic skater ever to accomplish two perfect triple-triple jumps in the same program.

When the judges' scores rolled in, a deafening roar went up from the crowd. Cameras zoomed in, showing Sarah and her coach on their knees, hugging each other and shrieking. Then Sarah's coach pressed Sarah's face in her hands and said, "You just won the gold medal in the Olympics!"

One day in heaven, you will experience a ceremony something like that. You will have finished your race. The time to receive the judge's reward will have arrived. It will be the biggest moment of your life....

And God wants it to be the *best* moment of your life!

That's what this book has been about. And today's Scripture passage contains some final, parting advice. In fact, did you notice it sounds a lot like a speech a coach might give just prior to an Olympic competition?

Like Paul, the writer of Hebrews pictured the life of faith as an athletic contest. He reminds us that the grandstands in heaven are packed, the crowds are watching, and the pressure is on! Then he gives believers invaluable pointers for winning our race:

1. *Lay aside everything that hinders you and the sin that entangles.* Serious athletes know that many things can slow them down and rule out their chances of winning—heavy clothing, poor eating or sleeping routines, and distractions or snares of any kind. In a disciple's race, nothing will slow you down, trip you up, and cause you to miss the prize like sin will.

Lay it aside today by confessing it to Jesus. John wrote, "If we confess our sins, He is faithful and just to forgive us our sins and to cleanse us from all unrighteousness" (1 John 1:9).

2. *Run with perseverance the race that is set before you.* On the walls of the Olympic Training Center in Colorado Springs is a motto: "Persistence is an invisible living strategy in all champions." We build our endurance when we do the right thing over and over—regardless of how we feel that day. Sometimes perseverance is as simple as just not giving up. Paul wrote, "And let us not grow weary while doing good, for in due season we shall reap if we do not lose heart" (Galatians 6:9).

But notice that you only have to run the race "marked out" for *you.* Your race is different from mine. And the race that is marked out for you was uniquely created for you, and you are uniquely gifted and called to win it.

3. *Fix your eyes on Jesus.* Any athlete will tell you that where you fix your eyes is critical. When Sarah Hughes turns herself into a spinning human top, she keeps her balance by focusing her eyes on exactly the same spot with each turn. In the same way, Jesus is the mark we fix our eyes on. He is our source of help and He is at the center of our reason for running. Jude wrote that Jesus *"is able to keep you from stumbling, and to present you faultless before the presence of His glory with exceeding joy"* (Jude 1:24).

If you've become convinced that you've misused your life and it will take a miracle to win God's "Well done," remember the One who will judge your race. He is at the finish line waiting for you, praying for you, eagerly anticipating giving you your reward (Revelation 22:12).

And His example is to run "for the joy set before Him." Serve Him fully today and every day *just for the joy of it*. And you can expect a wonderful reward from His loving hands.

MY REWARDS JOURNAL: *"Dear Lord, today I fix my eyes on You. Give me strength and wisdom as I run my race of faith. I choose to lay aside these sins that are entangling me."*

In this you greatly rejoice, though now for a little while, if need be, you have been grieved by various trials, that the genuineness of your faith, being much more precious than gold that perishes, though it is tested by fire, may be found to praise, honor, and glory at the revelation of Jesus Christ, whom having not seen you love. Though now you do not see Him, yet believing, you rejoice with joy inexpressible and full of glory, receiving the end of your faith—the salvation of your souls.

1 PETER 1:6–9

Now may the God of hope fill you with all joy and peace in believing, that you may abound in hope by the power of the Holy Spirit.

ROMANS 15:13

NOTES

1. Randy Alcorn uses the Dot and Line illustration in his book *The Treasure Principle* (Sisters, Ore.: Multnomah Publishers, 2001).
2. As quoted in Rick Howard and Jamie Lash, *This Was Your Life!* (Grand Rapids, Mich.: Chosen Books, 1998), 94–5.
3. Ibid.
4. Ibid.
5. Mark Buchanan, *Your God Is Too Safe* (Sisters, Ore.: Multnomah Publishers, 2001), 184.
6. C. S. Lewis, *The Last Battle* (New York: Harper Collins, 1994).
7. C. S. Lewis, *The Weight of Glory* (San Francisco: Harper San Francisco, 2001).

New companion products for
A Life God Rewards™

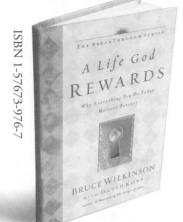

The BreakThrough Series, Book One
The Prayer of Jabez™

ISBN 1-57673-733-0

- #1 *New York Times* bestseller
- 11 million in print!
- www.prayerofjabez.com
- Book of the Year 2001 & 2002!

"Fastest selling book of all time."
—Publisher Weekly

The BreakThrough Series, Book Two
Secrets of the Vine™

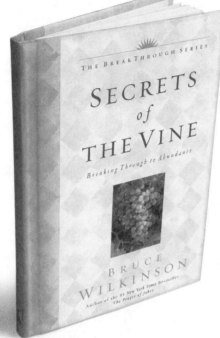

- ISBN 1-57673-975-9
- Over 3 Million in Print!
- www.thebreakthroughseries.com

• **Secrets of the Vine Audiocassette**	ISBN 1-57673-977-5
• **Secrets of the Vine Audio CD**	ISBN 1-57673-908-2
• **Secrets of the Vine Leather Edition**	ISBN 1-57673-876-0
• **Secrets of the Vine Journal**	ISBN 1-57673-960-0
• **Secrets of the Vine Devotional**	ISBN 1-57673-959-7
• **Secrets of the Vine Bible Study**	ISBN 1-57673-972-4
• **Secrets of the Vine Bible Study: Leader's Edition**	ISBN 1-57673-973-2
• **Secrets of the Vine Gift Edition**	ISBN 1-57673-915-5
• **Secrets of the Vine for Teens**	ISBN 1-57673-922-8